The Art of Interaction

What HCI Can Learn from

Interactive Art

Synthesis Lectures on Human-Centered Informatics

Editor
John M. Carroll, *Penn State University*

Human-Centered Informatics (HCI) is the intersection of the cultural, the social, the cognitive, and the aesthetic with computing and information technology. It encompasses a huge range of issues, theories, technologies, designs, tools, environments, and human experiences in knowledge work, recreation and leisure activity, teaching and learning, and the potpourri of everyday life. The series publishes state-of-the-art syntheses, case studies, and tutorials in key areas. It shares the focus of leading international conferences in HCI.

© Springer Nature Switzerland AG 2022

Reprint of original edition © Morgan & Claypool 2018

The Art of Interaction: What HCI Can Learn from Interactive Art
Ernest Edmonds

ISBN: 978-3-031-01094-1 Paperback
ISBN: 978-3-031-02222-7 eBook
ISBN: 978-3-031-00202-1 Hardcover

DOI: 10.1007/978-3-031-02222-7

A Publication in the Springer series
SYNTHESIS LECTURES ON HUMAN-CENTERED INFORMATICS #39
Series Editor: John M. Carroll, Penn State University

Series ISSN 1946-7680 Print 1946-7699 Electronic

The Art of Interaction

What HCI Can Learn from Interactive Art

Ernest Edmonds
De Montfort University

SYNTHESIS LECTURES ON HUMAN-CENTERED INFORMATICS #39

ABSTRACT

What can Human-Computer Interaction (HCI) learn from art? How can the HCI research agenda be advanced by looking at art research? How can we improve creativity support and the amplification of that important human capability? This book aims to answer these questions. Interactive art has become a common part of life as a result of the many ways in which the computer and the Internet have facilitated it. HCI is as important to interactive art as mixing the colours of paint are to painting. This book reviews recent work that looks at these issues through art research. In interactive digital art, the artist is concerned with how the artwork behaves, how the audience interacts with it, and, ultimately, how participants experience art as well as their degree of engagement. The values of art are deeply human and increasingly relevant to HCI as its focus moves from product design towards social benefits and the support of human creativity. The book examines these issues and brings together a collection of research results from art practice that illuminates this significant new and expanding area. In particular, this work points towards a much-needed critical language that can be used to describe, compare and frame research in HCI support for creativity.

KEYWORDS

human-computer interaction, interactive art, practice-based research, experience, engagement

To Emma (in memoriam)

and Robert, Meroë, Emma, Catriona, Lulu, and Eric.

Contents

Acknowledgements

This book originated from a keynote talk given to the Create10 conference held in Edinburgh in 2010: "The art of interaction", *Proceedings of Create10*, Edinburgh 2010. https://ewic.bcs.org/content/ConWebDoc/36532. (The original presentation can be viewed at https://www.youtube.com/watch?v=-W5MzJY_QU4.) Thanks are expressed to the organisers of the conference and Michael Smyth, in particular, for inviting me. A version of this paper was subsequently published in the journal *Digital Creativity* ("The art of interaction", *Digital Creativity*, 21:4, 2011. 257–264, DOI: 10.1080/14626268.2010.556347).

The book also draws on my chapter "Interactive art", in Candy, L. and Edmonds, E. A. (2011). *Interacting: Art, Research and the Creative Practitioner*. Libri Press, Oxford, pp. 18–32.

I am very grateful to my students and collaborators whose work I have explicitly drawn on: Stephen Bell, Zafer Bilda, Andrew Bluff, Matthew Connell, Stroud Cornock, Gina Czarnecki, Brigid Costello, Mark Fell, Francesca Franco, Andrew Johnston, Lizzie Muller, and Mike Quantrill. I am equally grateful to the many other students and collaborators with whom I have worked over the years, all of whom have helped me understand interactive art, HCI, and the relationship between the two. For many stimulating conversations that have informed my thinking, I am indebted to Margaret Boden, Gerhard Fischer, John Gero, Tom Hewett, Ben Shneiderman, and the many members of the art and HCI communities who have encouraged and influenced me.

I am grateful for the thoughtful suggestions made by the reviewers of my first draft of this book. Finally, I would like to thank Linda Candy for her advice and suggestions about the text and, above all, for the unfailing support that she has offered over many years.

CHAPTER 1

Introduction

Interactive art has become a common part of life as a result of the many ways in which the computer and the Internet have facilitated it. Human-Computer Interaction (HCI) is as important to interactive art making as the colours of paint are to painting. It is not that HCI and art share goals. It is just that much of the knowledge of HCI and its methods can contribute to interactive art making. This means that artists have been taking a very serious interest in HCI, including as part of their research activities. They have discovered some interesting things that can contribute to HCI. In learning from art, it is important to take the relevant value systems into account and, as art is deeply human, I will come at HCI from a very human perspective. I will not be discussing how to design products that will do well in the market. I will show how art can help HCI in its endeavour to enrich life and expand our understanding of human experience of interaction. This book reviews recent work in the area of art research and proposes contributions that these make to HCI.

Figure 1.1: *Shaping Space*, Ernest Edmonds. Site Gallery Sheffield 2012. Photo by Robert Edmonds, 2012.

In interactive digital art, the artist is concerned with how the artwork behaves, how the audience interacts with it and, ultimately, in participants' experiences and their degree of engagement. In this book, I examine these issues and bring together a collection of research results and art practice experiences that help to illuminate this significant new and expanding area. In particular, I suggest that this work points towards a much-needed critical language that can be used both to describe, compare, and discuss interactive systems art and to frame research in HCI, particularly in relation to support for creativity.

This book is, in essence, a lecture. It is written as such and so covers basic background material, some of which most readers will know. However different readers will know different parts of that background. For some, the historical context sections might readily be skipped, depending on the reader's knowledge. As with all good lectures, the intention is not just to impart information, not even primarily to impart information. The intention is to stimulate thinking about creativity and the future of HCI and to encourage further reading and exploration. At times my text is informal and I do not shy away from expressing opinion that, as yet, I cannot back up with hard evidence. Stimulating questions in the reader's mind is as important in this lecture as providing answers. The biggest question that I pose is: How best can HCI researchers learn from interactive art?

Digital art is increasingly interactive. Some of it is built on notions that come from computer games and much of it is intended to engage the audience in some form of interactive experience that is a key element in the aesthetics of the art.

This book reviews recent work that looks at the design of interactive systems in the art context. The concerns in HCI of experience design and understanding user engagement are especially relevant ones. We are not so much concerned with task analysis, error prevention, or task completion times as with issues such as pleasure, play, and long-term engagement.

In interactive digital art, the artist is concerned with how the artwork behaves, how the audience interacts with it (and possibly with one another through it) and, ultimately, in participant experience and their degree of engagement. In one sense, these issues have always been part of the artist's world but in the case of interactive art they have become both more explicit and more prominent within the full canon of concern.

Whilst HCI in its various forms can offer results that at times help the artist, the concerns in interactive art go beyond traditional HCI. Hence, we need to focus on issues that are in part new to, or emerging in, HCI research.

As is well known to HCI practitioners, we do not have a simple cookbook of recipes for interaction and experience design. Rather, we have methods that involve research and evaluation with users as part of the design process. The implications of this point for art practice are, in themselves, interesting. The art-making process needs to accommodate some form of audience research within what has often been a secret and private activity.

This book looks at these issues and brings together a collection of research results and art practice experiences that together help to illuminate this significant new and expanding area. I provide a set of case studies in interactive art research to help guide the reader on that further journey. I also include an extended description of my own journey. On the way I cover a little history, both of HCI and of art. I hope that HCI people might find an expanded way of looking at art—and learn from it—and also that artists might see a new way of looking at HCI.

CHAPTER 2

A Little HCI History

2.1 THE NAME HCI ITSELF

Human-Computer Interaction (HCI) is a relatively new field that is always changing. Even its name has gone through many transformations. Of course the advocates of each new name wish to imply some shift of focus or scope for the subject, as indeed has happened.

When I first worked in the field it was known as Man-Machine Interface, or a branch of Ergonomics or Human Factors (terms which still survive). Naturally, it turned out that the machines that mattered most to us were computers, so we started to talk about the Man-Computer Interface. Eventually, even the ground-breaking *International Journal of Man Machine Studies* (IJMMS, 2017) had to admit not only that we were concerned with computers but that the climate of opinion no longer accepted "man" as a generic term for all human beings. The journal moved with the times and changed its name to the *International Journal of Human-Computer Studies*.

Having moved on to using the phrase Human-Computer Interface, we then saw that it was not the object, the interface, that was the main concern but it was actually the process of interaction. The name of the field then moved to Human-Computer Interaction or, in the case of the important society the Association for Computing Machinery (ACM), Computer-Human Interaction. The ACM term removed a risk of ambiguity that some people were worried about. The subject is not concerned with computers that are human like (human computers) but about interaction between humans and computers.

The next move was based on the recognition that a really key element of the area was "design". Within the design community it is well recognised that many aspects transfer across domains, whilst others are quite specific. In our case, for example, interaction brings specific design concerns. So we now have a large body of work that goes under the heading of Interaction Design. Obviously, this does not cover all of HCI as it excludes, for example, studies of interaction behaviour that do not have direct design application. However, it is generally seen as another variant name in the field of HCI.

Just as once we moved from "interface" to "interaction", people have come to understand that the "experience" of interaction is often the key issue that we need to consider. Just think of Steve Jobs and the innovations he brought to the market at Apple (Isaacson, 2011). The result is another shift, this time to Experience Design. Some people will argue that designing experiences is not quite what is being done and that terms like Design for Experience or Experience-Centered Design capture it more accurately. In any case, Interaction Design is important in this book and will figure as such.

We could go on, and these changes and transformations certainly will in the future. For this book, however, from now on I will use the term HCI in its most general sense to cover the range of work named in these many different ways: human computer interface, interaction design, experience design. etc.

2.2   FROM EASY-TO-USE TO USER EXPERIENCE

In 1947, writing about programming the EDVAC computer, Mauchly said "Any machine coding system should be judged quite largely from the point of view of how easy it is for the operator to obtain results" (Mauchly, 1973). Ease of use was a concern in computing from the very beginning. Of course, Mauchly's user was the "operator" or, as we would say today, the programmer. Quite a bit of HCI research has in the past been directed at the programmer and the design of programming languages, so he was hardly alone in adopting this focus.

The late Brian Shackel's paper "Ergonomics for a computer" was published in *Design* in 1959 and can be seen as the start of the serious consideration of research in HCI (Shackel, 1959). It brought our attention to the need to include human factors into computer science research.

The next important steps were very much concerned with the "interface" as was indicated in the early names mentioned above. Ivan Sutherland completed his Ph.D. in 1963 in which he presented Sketchpad and many of the founding ideas of interactive computer graphics that are still relevant today (Sutherland, 1963). Shortly afterwards, Doug Engelbart invented the mouse (Engelbart, 1967). Taken together these advances in the computer interface laid down the foundations of modern interactive computing.

An important conceptual moment for HCI was Alan Kay's idea of the Dyna-Book, a small tablet-like computer designed to be used by children (Kay, 1972). It was way beyond any engineering capability available at that time but provided a vision of the future. As Mike Richards put it, when reviewing the iPhone in 2008, "After a forty-year delay, Alan Kay's DynaBook might just have arrived" (Richards, 2008). Perhaps, really, the DynaBook has arrived in the form of the iPad, which, after all, was put on the shelf for a little while once Steve Jobs realised that a smaller version could be revolutionary: the iPhone (Isaacson, 2011: 468).

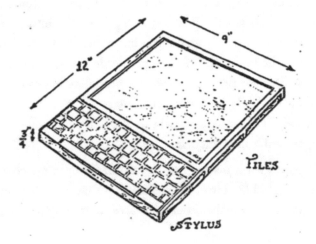

Figure 2.1: Alan Kay's sketch of DynaBook. Courtesy Alan Kay.

That Alan Kay's vision of a machine that would be easy, natural, for children to use can surely be seen in the iPhone and iPad. It is commonplace to see very young children, of two or even one, manipulating these machines by pointing and swiping. Progress towards this end was made much stronger by the foundation of Xerox PARC (the Xerox Palo Alto Research Center, now PARC) in 1970. This hothouse of computing development was driven by a general application led strategy—focused on the office—and by drawing in all that was innovative and promising, particularly, but not only, in the HCI area.

Also in 1970, Brian Shackel founded the HUSAT (Human Sciences and Advanced Technology) Research Institute at Loughborough University in the UK, which became a major center for HCI research (Shackel, 1992). Then, in 1976, SIGGRAPH held the UODIGS workshop on "User-oriented design of interactive graphics systems" (Treu, 1976). In the same year a conference on "Computing and People" was held in Leicester in the UK (Parkin, 1977). In 1978, the ACM Special Interest Group on Social and Behavioural Computing (SIGSOC) ran a panel at the ACM Conference on "People-oriented Systems: When and How?" So, a process that would lead to the first American conference on human-computer interaction in 1981, "The Joint Conference on Easier and More Productive Use of Computer Systems," had started, and SIGSOC was transformed into SIGCHI. Note that the main preoccupations at this time were mostly ease of use and the consequential benefit to productivity.

Meanwhile, some people were dreaming about the magic of the DynaBook, of children "playing" with computers, and with the user's enjoyment. A famous critical event was the visit by Steve Jobs, and others from Apple, to Xerox PARC in 1979 (Isaacson, 2011: 96). They saw the prototype machines with bitmap displays, using a mouse and emulating the use of paper and printing on the screen. Jobs was not slow to say that this was the future and that Apple needed to produce it, albeit at a tiny fraction of the cost. This was the start of the commercial move towards DynaBook and the 1984 launch of the Apple Macintosh computer.

In the second CHI conference, held in 1982, Tom Malone presented a paper about designing enjoyable user interfaces.

> "In this paper, I will discuss two questions: (1) Why are computer games so captivating? And (2) How can the features that make computer games captivating be used to make other interfaces interesting and enjoyable to use?" (Malone, 1982).

This might be seen as the start of the research effort to look at user engagement and enjoyment as significant research and design issues.

Naturally, a concern for engagement and enjoyment points to the need to look hard at user experience. Kevin Biles' 1994 paper in *Computer Graphics*, "Notes on Experience Design", set the agenda:

> "Technology, no matter what it is, isn't the entertainment. The integration of technology needs to be seamless in an attraction, always letting the story and the overall experience take the front seat" (Biles, 1994).

The HCI trend from "ease of use" to "user experience" is the human side of the trend described by Jonathan Grudin as "tool to partner" (Grudin, 2016). Much of Grudin's more detailed history can be interpreted in this human-oriented way, but, as I will show, there are trends that hardly focus on the computer side of HCI at all. In that respect, one particularly significant issue is embodiment. In the broad sense, this is concerned with understanding interaction in the physical and social context in which it takes place (Dourish, 2001). The concern for embodiment in art is sometimes very specifically about interaction that takes the body and movement fully into account, as in the case of dancers and performers. See the case that I discuss in Section 5.4.

In the next section, I will describe how recent developments have been bringing HCI closer to the human values found in art by concentrating on the support that can be offered to enhancing human creativity.

2.3   ON TO ENHANCING CREATIVITY

An interest in creativity began to flower in the Artificial Intelligence, Cognitive Science, and Design communities at the end of the 1980s. The "First International Conference on Computational and Cognitive Models of Creative Design" was held on a Great Barrier Reef island in 1989 and turned into a regular series (Gero and Maher, 1989). Margaret Boden (1991) published her book, *The Creative Mind: Myths and Mechanisms,* in 1991. The main thrust of this kind of work was in building and critiquing computational models of creative processes, but some designers and members of the HCI community also took a strong interest. They had a different focus, that of envisaging how computational systems might support and enhance human creativity.

This development seemed a natural extension to the HCI concerns for engagement and enjoyment. We were no longer locked into an HCI focus that emphasised work (the "easier and more productive use of computer systems" of the first CHI). Instead, interest was growing in entertainment, art, and pleasure. The values had changed. Of course, it turned out that a considerable amount of work involves creativity. Creativity in the Design domain was first to receive significant attention. It was found that the older emphasis on work was, in fact, on *routine* tasks: copy editing, for example, rather than writing a screen play.

In 1993, the first Creativity and Cognition conference was held at Loughborough University in the UK. This conference, and the many that followed, took a strong multidisciplinary approach in what was initially an exploration of a possible new area:

> "…the cognitive modeling of creativity, the empirical study of the creative process and the theoretical reflection upon its characteristics are of concern to everyone involved whether artist, designer, philosopher, cognitive scientist, or computer scientist" (Edmonds, 1993).

By the 1996 meeting of this conference series (as it had become) the primary goal of supporting human creativity became clear:

> "The design of creativity supporting computer systems is now firmly on the research agenda" (Candy and Edmonds, 1996).

Creativity had become an HCI research issue.

As mentioned above, Loughborough University, where the Creativity and Cognition conference series began, was an early and very strong HCI research center. Hence, the conference series developed in an HCI climate and by 1999 it had been adopted by ACM SIGCHI as a sponsored conference, which it remains today. Since then the range of conferences and publications in the area has expanded vastly. Funding bodies have also taken an interest. In the late 1990s, the UK's Engineering and Physical Sciences Research Council added the topic of supporting creativity to its definition of interesting areas of HCI. In 2005, the U.S.'s National Science Foundation (NSF) sponsored a high-level workshop on Creativity Support Tools in Washington DC (Shneiderman et al., 2006).

The NSF workshop can be seen as a pivotal event in relation to HCI and creativity: "This U.S. National Science Foundation sponsored workshop brought together 25 research leaders and graduate students to share experiences, identify opportunities, and formulate research challenges. Two key outcomes emerged:

1. encouragement to evaluate creativity support tools through multidimensional in-depth longitudinal case studies; and

2. formulation of 12 principles for design of creativity support tools" (Shneiderman et al., 2006).

The evaluation outcome was to recommend that the way forward should focus on "multiple metrics and evaluation techniques based on long-term in-depth observations and interviews over weeks and months with individuals and groups." Twelve principles were identified that provide a valuable check list.

1. Support exploration.

2. Low threshold, high ceiling, and wide walls.

3. Support many paths and many styles.

4. Support collaboration.

5. Support open interchange.

6. Make it as simple as possible—and maybe even simpler.

7. Choose black boxes carefully.

8. Invent things that you would want to use yourself.

9. Balance user suggestions with observation and participatory processes.

10. Iterate, iterate—then iterate again.

11. Design for designers.

12. Evaluate your tools.

Art has increasingly appeared in the topic lists of computing conferences. For example, the ACM conference CHI, has recently embraced art within its scope, i.e., holding a paper session on "Art, music, and movement" in 2011[1] and featuring both the Digital Arts and the Games and Entertainment communities in 2012. By 2016, it held its first fully fledged exhibition of interactive art.[2] Thus, a new agenda was added to HCI research that addressed the challenge of how to enable people to become more creative in whatever pursuit they followed.

Much of the work referred to is concerned with what is sometimes called "every-day creativity." We will see, however, in a later chapter, that the creative arts and the kind of exceptional creativity that particularly excites our admiration has much to teach us in HCI and in enhancing that everyday creativity.

2.4   TOWARDS A NEW HCI VOCABULARY

In one sense, the vocabulary normally used within a subject defines its scope. If we look at the ACM CHI conferences, for example, we find that in the proceedings of the first meeting, in 1981, the word "creative" turns up once and the word "productive" turns up 95 times. In 2011, by contrast, "creative" occurs in 141 contributions, whereas "productive" is only used in 41. So we see a shift in interest in the community, as discussed previously, illustrated simply by the vocabulary used.

In a quick scan of the paper titles from 1981/82, I notice words such as:

- command
- programming
- explanation
- documentation
- friendliness
- lexicon
- performance
- effectiveness
- productive
- learning
- stress
- search
- thesaurus
- icon
- menu
- scrolling

In 2011, in a similar scan, I see:

- sharing
- persuasive
- creative
- reflection
- emotion
- engaging
- experience
- expressive

- aesthetics
- touch
- feel
- gesture
- sensing
- multitasking
- multimodal
- pointing

By 2017, I can add:

- harmony
- moods
- awareness
- presence

- empowered
- mindfulness
- empathy

One might say that there is a move from routine work and productive concerns to human and creative ones. The frequency of the use of the words "productive" and "creative" themselves in the CHI conferences changed from the 95 (productive) to 1 (creative) in 1981 to, typically, parity by 2016.

These may only be word lists, however, behind them we can see the research agenda in HCI. The research questions that are being addressed are framed using these words. Of course, my scan of the literature was hardly rigorous, but the drift is clear. Today, we live in a world much more concerned with human creativity, with emotion, experience, and feelings, than we did in 1981. Artists are at the center of the development of new creative paths. That is why the argument of this book, this lecture, is that it is increasingly valuable for the HCI world to look at and to learn from the world of art. As I live in both of those worlds, and can demonstrate the value of HCI to art, I think that I am in a good position to assert that the benefits are reciprocal. I will elaborate on this in Chapter 3.

CHAPTER   3

Learning from Interactive Art

3.1   A LITTLE ART HISTORY

We may often think in terms of emotion and feeling when we look at, or listen to, art. In the theatre we may see a production that exudes magic. But the works we see and hear are, of course, made by careful and informed hard work, certainly not by magic. The image of a mad genius pouring out their anguish or joy has little to do with the reality of making art. Vincent van Gough may have had problems, but he was a highly learned man who was very deliberate about the way he constructed his paintings.[3] In what follows, I will look at art practice, how artists work, rather than at the artworks that they produce.

Just as in any other walk of life, the artist must conduct at least personal research. For example, an artist might need to work out which kind of paint will provide the best colour range. In fact, art practice can be seen as akin to research in that each artwork is a kind of experiment from which the artist learns, and that influences what is done next. Many artists share this attitude whether they use the word "research" or not. In his classic book *The Story of Art*, Gombrich even headed his chapter on the first half of the 20th century with the title "Experimental Art" (Gombrich, 1972). The art historian Stephen Bann explained this view of art practice:

> "my own definition of the experimental painter is that he is committed to a particular *path* of controlled activity, of which the works which he produces remain as evidence. In other words, the direction in which the artist moves is at least as important as the individual statements which record the track that he has taken." (Bann, 1970)

From the early years of the 20th century, explicit and public reference to research became an important part of some artist's lives.

The work of Russian artists around the time of the 1917 revolutions was of critical importance. Amongst them, Kazimir Malevich (famous for the *Black Square*—and much more) was one of the leading figures (Nakov, 2002). In late 1919 he joined Chagall, El Lissitzky, and others on the staff of a new art school, the People's School of Art in Vitebsk. Here, he began to introduce scientific research and its methods in

---

[3]   Just browse the letters: http://vangoghletters.org/vg/letters.html.

art education, perhaps partly influenced by the dominance of science and technology in the thinking of the new Russian regime. In 1923, he became Director of the Petrograd Museum of Artistic Culture. It was not long before he gave it a new name: The Research Institute of Artistic Labor, which "carries out research…in the area of contemporary art…*including the*…application of art methods." So the explicit role of research—with a strong science and technological bias—was firmly to be seen in the art world (Kachurin, 2013).

As the Russian artist's influence spread, the idea of art as "visual research" grew. The use of mathematics was championed, particularly by Max Bill. In 1949 he argued that:

> "… it is possible to evolve a new form of art in which the artist's work could be founded to quite a substantial degree on a mathematical line of approach…" (Bill, 1949).

The concern here was with the structural underpinning of the art. Geometry, for example, is primarily the study of visual forms from a certain point of view. It is not surprising that what we learn from Geometry can be valuable to the visual artist.

Figure 3.1: Max Bill. *Ardiv III*, screenprint, 1972 (collection of Ernest Edmonds).

In Paris, in the 1960s, GRAV, Groupe de Recherche d'Art Visuel (Research Art Group) was a significant group of artists who, like Malevich, were very explicit about embracing research as a part of art practice (Galimberti, 2015).

At the same time, art and computing were coming together: an exhibition of "algorithmic art" was held in Stuttgart, another in New York. The landmark exhibition, Cybernetic Serendipity, was held at the Institute of Creative Art (I.C.A.) in London (Reichardt, 1968). The Computer Arts Society[4] was formed, also in London. Experiments in Art and Technology (E.A.T) was founded in New York[5], and so on.

Then, in 1970, a conference and exhibition on Computer Graphics was held at Brunel University near London.[6] It included a computer art section and was also inclusive of what was to become HCI. By 1974, ACM SIGGRAPH (the Special Interest Group on Computer Graphics), was active and in 1981 started including an art exhibition within its main conference. The emphasis was, naturally, on graphical art objects generated by computer rather than on anything particularly concerned with HCI.

During the 1970s, what became known as Practice-Based Ph.D.s began in the UK. These were research degrees in which practice played a significant part and in which artefacts, for example paintings, could be submitted with the thesis for examination. Many of these involved the use of digital technology. These Ph.D.s and other research conducted in this practice-based mode is particularly instructive in the context this book. I will elaborate on that in Section 3.3.

3.2   LEARNING FROM RESEARCH IN ART

The key HCI issue that we came to in Chapter 2 was the problem of supporting people to be more creative. The implied research required is about understanding creative processes. This includes the contexts in which they flourish and the constraints that help or hinder successful results. Hidden behind this research is a requirement to evaluate creative processes and, hence, a need to determine the success or failure of their outcomes. Taken as a whole, we can see that this is a particularly difficult research challenge.

So, how can art help? Well, it is common in science to look at what are known as "boundary conditions" or "boundary cases". We can often learn more by studying the most extreme conditions than we can by studying just the normal everyday ones. For example, vision, or how we see and understand the world around us, is quite a difficult topic. One way in which it has been advanced is by looking at situations where the

---

[4]   http://computer-arts-society.com.

[5]   http://www.fondation-langlois.org/html/e/page.php?NumPage=306.

[6]   CG70: International Symposium Computer Graphics, Brunel University, UK.

process goes wrong. This is done, for example, by studying visual illusions, where we can find clues about how the process works (Gregory, 1974).

In Figure 3.2, most people will see the left-hand horizontal line to be longer than the right-hand one. In fact, they are the same length. This illusion gives us a clue. It suggests that we might be imposing an expectation of perspective on the picture and so we see the left hand line as further away than the right hand one and, hence, we think it is longer. Thus, our visual perception is probably influenced by expectations of seeing a 3D world, and 2D representations of it. We see the influence of the laws of perspective.

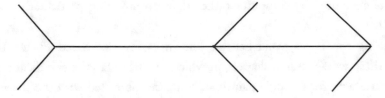

Figure 3.2: Illusion (Müller-Lyer).

Another example of looking at boundary cases was Csikszentmihalyi's work on human creativity (Csikszentmihalyi, 1996). Instead of looking at the creative acts that all of us take on most days, he looked at Nobel Prize winners. What was special about them? He found that they had typically put in years of hard work before they had that famous flash of inspiration. They knew quite a lot about and around the area where they made their, possibly quite unexpected, discoveries. They had also experienced and survived failure or difficulty early on in life more than most of us. From this we can propose that, for everyone, creativity might be fostered by preparation or practice and by developing a tolerance of failure. Perhaps most of us do not try hard enough in the first place and give up too easily the first time we get it wrong.

We are considering the problem of supporting people to be more creative. Taking a "boundary case" approach, it is interesting to look at supporting clearly creative people in well-known creative tasks. Artists practicing their art often fall directly into this category. How does this help? Well, artists are very demanding and reject any tool or help that does not precisely serve their purpose. They represent a boundary case in the need for creativity support and so, by looking at them, we can obtain a clear picture of the issues. If we look at more ordinary cases, although the same results will probably show up, they will not be so easy to spot. Of course, this view is based on the idea that artists are normal people with all of the normal characteristics. It is just that they are particularly good at or committed to their form of creativity. If, on the other hand, you take the view that an artist is a god-like genius, quite different to the rest of us, then this argument does not work. However, I do not take that view and nor do many people in the 21st century.

In Section 3.4, I will concentrate on artists who are making interactive art. This is even more special in our context than art in general. In interactive art a more accurate term for "the audience" is "the participants". These participants interact with the artwork in ways that, in some sense or other, engages them in a creative way. So, there are two layers of creativity here. The artist is being creative in making artworks that encourage the participants to engage in creative experiences. The interactive artist is a boundary case both in the sense of being a very creative practitioner and an extreme case of a person designing for participant (user) creative experience.

As well as providing interesting boundary cases, studies of and by interactive artists provide a significant opportunity for tackling the problem of supporting people to be more creative. These artists are particularly demanding "users" and, as such, highlight the problems that need to be overcome for us all. The complexities of interactive artworks and their successful design and implementation have led some artists in that area to conduct sizable research projects about interaction. The results of these projects can provide many pointers to the way forward for HCI in the development of creativity support. We will come to this a little later, but first, it will be helpful to say a few things about interactive art itself.

3.3   PRACTICE-BASED ART RESEARCH

Research within and about art practice is relatively new compared to the broad area of science, as is HCI itself. Psychology and Ergonomics were foundation subjects for HCI and so research methods traditional in those areas have frequently been adopted. Art, however, offers a different model, one that is also found in design. Although design may not have been enthusiastically grasped in the early days, it is also a foundation subject for HCI.

At this point let us consider art research in a little more detail. The situation is varied as different countries have taken different positions.[7] We can safely take the

---

[7]   Regulations for practice-based Ph.D.s that allowed an artefact of some description to be submitted with a thesis were introduced in the UK Polytechnics from the early 1970s and remain available in the universities that they later became. Other countries, such as Australia, have also provided this option for some time. There are a few universities in the U.S. that have such a route and interest is growing.

research degree, the Ph.D., as a touchstone for research standards and conventions. After all, the Ph.D. is the key degree that trains people for research and so, by its very nature, embodies the relevant conventions that are expected. The innovation in research methods most familiar to the art community are those of the "practice-based research" degree. In this model, the practice itself is the basis for reflection and study, both contributing to the research. When a Ph.D. is submitted, an artefact of some sort may be included with (or at times even instead of) a thesis. The basic premise is that the process of making the artefact and/or the information embodied in it is critical to understanding the research results (Candy and Edmonds, 2018).

Clearly, this is not a form of "pure" basic research: it is concerned with practice and, as such, with application more than theory. This is not to say that theory cannot be significant or that it might not form an important element in the research contribution. The emphasis, however, is on contributions to informing practice rather than improving understanding and theory alone. The relationship between theory and practice in this kind of research is discussed by Edmonds and Candy (2010). A broader argument for rethinking traditional research methods so as to bring application and practice to the fore is in Ben Shneiderman's recent book (Shneiderman, 2016).

Put simply, practice-based research in art is an original investigation made in order to gain new knowledge by means of practice, through making. Its results are demonstrated by a combination of textual description and artefact. In 1995, Bruce Archer made the very clear point that "There are circumstances where the best or only way to shed light on a proposition, a principle, a material, a process or a function is to attempt to construct something, or to enact something, calculated to explore, embody or test it" (Archer, 1995).

It has proven important to make a clear distinction between pure practice and practice-based research. Practice itself does not constitute research (other than in the "personal" mode) but practice, as performed by artists, is a life-long pursuit that might be thought of as a research project as discussed in Section 3.1. Each artefact made is a kind-of experiment, the evaluation of which informs the next act of making.

It is important to remember what "research" is in the context of public dissemination, academic life, and HCI, in particular. Research is an activity that seeks new knowledge—new to the world. It disseminates that knowledge for public scrutiny and comment, including making very clear what methods were used to obtain it. This means that when research results are published or a Ph.D. is submitted it is normal to expect to see a justification of the claim that it is new—a survey of existing results, for example—and a description of what is new and how it was obtained. The natural way to do this is in a text. However, in art and design research it has been found that at times the results can only be understood fully by displaying the key artefact(s) involved. Although all research must be disseminated, original and contextualised it does not have to be presented purely in the form of text.

The role of the artefact in practice-based research is not just as an illustration of the point being made. It is integral to the results and often to the research process itself. In my case, I recall being told by my Ph.D. supervisor that a diagram that I used to illustrate a point in a logical proof was not needed. He meant that it was possible (though perhaps hard) to understand that proof by just reading the mathematical description. I accepted that point and deleted the diagram. However, in the case of the art research that we are discussing the artefact, diagram—painting—symphony—performance, may be a critical thing to apprehend in order to fully grasp the results.

To take an HCI example, I suggest that the significance of direct manipulation (Shneiderman, 1982) would be very hard to appreciate without the experience of using it. Of course, the benefits can be described, experiments can be reported and a persuasive argument in its favor can be made but can we understand the point without moving the mouse and seeing it work? I suggest not. So it is with art.

The methods used in practice-based art research include all of those that we are familiar with, but add others. Perhaps most significant is reflection. Donald Schön introduced the concept of reflection in and on practice, where a professional worker thinks about what they do as they do it and find ways of improving both their understanding and their performance (Schön, 1983). This realisation of how the professional works has been adopted widely as an adjunct research method in various domains, including art and design. In order to move from an observation on practice to a research method, the requirement has been to ensure that the reflections are documented. So, the method used in art and design research might be best termed "documented reflection". This reflection is, of course, on everything that happens including what goes wrong, and what reaction is taken to problems, just as much as to what works well.

Practice-based research does not typically produce the highly reliable results that we see from controlled experiments, but it does provide answers to much bigger questions than such experiments can address. We have to choose between reliable answers to small questions, such as the best way to cut and paste, and good answers to big questions, such as how best to support the writing of a film script. Obviously, both extremes, and everything in between, matters, but my argument is that HCI research includes the big questions and hence that the practice-based research model is one to seriously consider.

3.4   INTERACTIVE ART[8]

Art becomes interactive when audience participation is an integral part of the artwork. Audience behaviour can cause the art itself to change. In making interactive art, the artist goes beyond considerations of how the work will look or sound. The way that it interacts with the audience is a crucial part of it. The core of the art is in the work's behaviour more than in any other aspect. The creative practice of an interactive artist is, therefore, quite different to that of a painter. A painting is static and so, in so far as a painter considers audience reaction, the perception of colour relationships, scale, figurative references, and so on will be of most interest. In the case of interactive art, however, the audience's behavioural response to the artwork's activity is what matters. Audience engagement is in terms of what they do, how they develop interactions with the piece, whether they experience pain or pleasure, and so on.

Perception is an active process (Norwich, 1982). Even when we stand still and look at Leonardo Da Vinci's *Mona Lisa*, our perceptual system, the part of the brain behind the eyes, is actively engaging with the painting. However, we do not change the painting in any way. As we look longer it may seem to change and we sometimes say that we "see more in it," but it is our perception of it that is changing. This change process is most often mentioned in relation to works such as those by Mark Rothko where, at first, it may seem as if there is nothing much to see, but the more we look, the more we perceive. Campbell-Johnston commented, "as you gaze into the [Rothko] canvases you see that their surfaces are modulated. Different patterns and intensities and tones emerge" (Campbell-Johnston, 2008). Marcel Duchamp went so far as to claim that the audience completes the artwork. The active engagement with the work by the viewer is the final step in the creative process. As he put it:

> "the spectator … adds his contribution to the creative act" (Duchamp, 1957).

From this perspective, audience engagement with an artwork is an essential part of the creative process. The audience is seen to join with the artist in making the work. This position became a particularly significant one for artists in the second half of the 20th century.

Since the 1960s, an increasing number of artists have been taking active engagement further. Most famously, in the period of the so-called "happenings", direct and physical audience participation became an integral part of the artwork or performance (Sandford, 1995). Situations were devised by the artists in which the audience was encouraged to physically engage and explicitly change the work. The audience partly

---

[8]   I have written an essay that discusses interactive art in detail, and which the reader is referred to for more information (Edmonds, 2011).

determines the nature of the artwork. Indeed, the activity of engagement became part of the artwork. Often with the help of electronics, members of the audience were able to touch an artwork and cause it to change. Art became interactive. See, for example, Frank Popper's book on the subject (Popper, 2007). Sometimes we talk about observably interactive art just to be clear that the interactive activity is not just in someone's head but can be seen in terms of movement, sound, or changing images.

Seen from this perspective, an interactive artwork can be partly described in terms of its behaviour. The nature of light that falls on a painting, the colour of the wall on which it is hung, and so on, certainly change how it looks. Physically, however, it is fixed. An interactive artwork, on the other hand, consists of a system that both changes within itself, where that change is apparent to an observer, and is influenced by the audience.

Most artists do not use the keyboard and/or mouse as input devices in their work. Apart from novel styles of interaction, they often use novel physical means of interaction. Another key point is that in interactive art, there is normally no simply defined task and so the interaction process is driven by creative exploration as often as by pre-set goals.

The computer, as a control device, can manage interactive processes in ways never seen before. Today, we are often hardly aware of the computers that we use at all. They operate our watches, our washing machines, our telephones, our cars, and a high percentage of the other devices that we use on a daily basis. It is not a big step, therefore, to find that the artworks that we engage with also sometimes have computers behind them.

There is another area in which interaction, or at least the use of computers, has brought changes to creative practice. The complexity of computer systems and the many sub-areas of specialist knowledge required for their full exploitation have increased the need for collaboration by the artist with other people. The artist today is often a member of a collaborative team and the role "artist" is even shifting to be applicable to the whole team or at least beyond one individual. A technical expert, for example, may often make creative contributions and may, as a result, be named as a co-author of the resulting artwork (Candy and Edmonds, 2002b). The collaboration may not be limited to technical matters. There is a need for research into human behaviour and this research may also be something that requires skilled input from an expert other than the artist and technologist/scientist themselves.

A significant feature is the nature of the collaboration between the roles of artist, researcher and technologist. It can be that one person performs all of these roles, but often a team is involved. Even then, the way that a team works can be quite varied.

However, the notion of the researcher and technologist being assistants to the artist is becoming less common. Partnerships are often formed in which the roles are spread across the team.

Here we consider three examples of such partnerships in art.

1. Christa Sommerer and Laurent Mignonneau

    Sommerer and Mignonneau have a substantial history of collaborating on interactive artworks based on artificial life (Sommerer and Mignonneau, 2009). Indeed, as early as 1992 they made a work, *Interactive Plant Growing*, that used real plants as the interface that participants touched or approached.

Figure 3.2: *Life Spaces II* by Sommener and Mignonneau, © Sommener and Mignonneau, 1999.

    A classic later example of their work is *Life Spaces II*, which was created in 1999. Physically, the work consists of a laptop computer on a stand in front a large projection screen. Virtual creatures, appear, grow, and move on the screen using artificial life concepts. Participants are invited to type text into the laptop (this work *does* use the keyboard, but for a very specific purpose) and, as they do, the text is used by the computer to generate new virtual creatures that enter the space. Participants can also type in text that becomes food for the creatures to eat.

"The creature's lifetime is not predetermined, rather it is influenced by how much it eats…a creature will starve when it does not eat enough text characters and ultimately die and sink to the ground…

Written text … is used as genetic code, and our text-to-form editor translates the written texts into three-dimensional autonomous creatures whose bodies, behaviours, interactions, and survival are solely based on their genetic code and the users' interactions" (Sommerer and Mignonneau, 2009: 107-8).

2. Sidney Fels and Kenji Mase

A successful interactive artwork that uses a direct relationship between the input and aspects of the output is *Iamascope*. In this case the input is through the analysis of images captured by a camera pointing at the participant. This work was a collaboration between Kenji Mase, a technologist deeply interested in creativity, and Sidney Fells, an artist who is also an accomplished computer scientist.

As the designers of this system describe it:

"The *Iamascope* is an interactive kaleidoscope, which uses computer video and graphics technology. In the Iamascope, the performer becomes the object inside the kaleidoscope and sees the kaleidoscopic image on a large screen in real time. The *Iamascope* is an example of using computer technology to develop art forms. As such, the *Iamascope* does not enhance functionality of some device or in other words, 'do any thing', rather, its intent is to provide a rich, aesthetic visual experience for the performer using it and for people watching the performance" (Fels and Mase, 1999).

The idea is that one member of the audience acts as "performer". An image-processing system detects certain body movements that they make (typically, waving their arms) and uses that to generate both kaleidoscopic-type image transformations of them and music. It is also intended to be interesting to other members of the audience who just watch the action, and it is!

As *Iamascope* demonstrates, experiencing interactive art can take many forms. The nature of play, for example, is often the subject of interactive art and so "game" and "artwork" can come together. The work must then engage the audience in playful behaviours. The aesthetic results, of course, may be important in other respects. Art is multi-layered, normally working at different levels simultaneously, and we certainly must not assume that the significance of playful art is limited to play itself.

Figure 3.3: *Iamascope* by Fels and Mase. Photo Linda Candy, 2000.

I will try to introduce some of these different layers and concerns in the Chapter 4, which presents some of my personal history of making and thinking about interactive art.

3. Gina Czarnecki and Mark Fell

Artist Gina Czarnecki worked on her interactive piece *Silvers Alter*, whilst on an artists' residency at Loughborough University. She was supported technically by Mark Fell, who is also an artist. Czarnecki explained that:

"The installation takes the form of a large back projection screen on which the human forms 'live'. These figures are changed by the audience's presence and movements in the space" (Candy and Edmonds, 2002c).

She elaborated:

"This piece is a development from *Stages Elements Humans*, a video installation commissioned for the *Year of Photography and Electronic Image, 1998*. It is based on issues surrounding genetic engineering and related scientific, technological and ethical concerns. It is an experimental observation of the development of consciousness and science. It raises a simple question: to what extent are we prepared to participate in all that we have made possible and that we aspire to make possible for ourselves? It gives the audience the power to create, eliminate and stare" (ibid).

Figure 3.4: Silvers Alter by Gina Czarnecki, 2002. Photo: the artist.

"I wanted to maintain the politics of the space in that the interaction between people within it was fundamental to how they engage with the technology and the ideas. To control the space people have to work together and to be so physically close to one another that they touch. The team suggested that instead of the audience selecting two figures independently before a third could form, they selected one and there was a constant 'last-born'. In order to change the evolution of the population this would then compromise the generational simplicity, but the interface would be far simpler, more obvious to understand for the audience whilst maintaining integrity of the ideas and the parallel interactivity of many people in the space" (ibid).

Unlike some other interactive artworks, such as the two preceding examples, *Silvers Alter* does not necessarily offer a pleasant experience. The participants are challenged and may feel uncomfortable as the interaction proceeds. We will see in the case study of Brigid Costello's work (Section 5.1) that there are many forms of interactive experience used in art and only some of them could be termed "pleasant."

CHAPTER 4

A Personal History

This chapter reviews the development of the frameworks for thinking and talking about interactive art that I developed in my personal practice over the last 50 years. It traces a number of paths taken, from an early simple direct notion of interaction through to communication between people through art systems and, more recently, interactive art for long-term engagement. The frameworks consist of an evolving set of concepts, over several dimensions, which are developing together with the practice of interactive art.

At the start of my journey as an artist, a number of technical issues arose that led to me proposing innovations in HCI. That were not always welcome, however; for example, when, in 1970, I found the need for the design and development process to be iterative, I found it hard to publish the ideas. One rejection letter said "If you don't know what you are going to do before you start, you shouldn't start." The paper eventually found a home in the General Systems world (Edmonds, 1974). A discussion of this and other innovations is given in Chapter 7 of Francesca Franco's book on my work (Franco, 2018). I leave the reader to think about the HCI implications as they read this history, but I will briefly present my thoughts at the end of the chapter.

A significant part of art making, for me, is the development of an understanding of the forms and material being used, what Cezanne called "a language and a logic" (Doran, 2001: 17). The language that the artist evolves is a language of form, of course: shapes, colours, textures, and so on. Such a language helps one think about and discuss the art. For example, although the key issues about an understanding of colour may be themselves embodied in artworks, it is also good to be able to name hue, saturation, intensity, etc. This helps in the thinking about colour that provides the context for using it.

The practice I discuss in this chapter is concerned with developing and exploring *interaction* in the context of art. It is concerned with the form, language, and logic of interaction. The frameworks discussed are sets of words that help in the development of interactive art in the same way that words such as hue and saturation help with the painting of colour. So the frameworks help to frame my thinking and hence my practice of interactive art and HCI. It is not surprising that they are always evolving.

4.1   INTERACTION AND THE COMPUTER

In the 1960s, although my art was primarily painting, I took an interest in "happenings", in which direct and physical audience participation became, at times, an integral part of the artwork. Allan Kaprow's *Eat*, for example, included amongst its props, fruit that the audience was invited to eat (Kirby, 1965). Artists devised situations in which the audience was meant to engage by actually taking part and so explicitly shape or create the artwork. It seemed to me that involving audiences explicitly in the creative process of art making was "in the air" at the time. In novel writing, for example, B.S. Johnson published *The Unfortunates*, which consisted of 27 sections, which, with the exception of the first and last, could be read in any order that the reader desired (Johnson, 1969). The visual artist Roy Ascott was working on a range of artworks that could be modified or re-arranged by the audience. He saw a potential for computers to enable the development of interaction in a number of ways, including what he termed "telematic art" (Ascott, 1966).

Thinking about audience engagement and interaction in the arts led me to consider those ideas more generally. Cybernetics, and the closely related study of Systems Theory, seemed to me to provide a rich set of concepts that helped us to think about change, interaction and living systems (von Bertalanffy, 1950; Wiener, 1965). Whilst the art has not been built by directly applying these scientific disciplines, many of the basic concepts, such as interactive systems and feedback, have influenced the development of the frameworks discussed below. I first became interested in exploring interaction within my art practice in the late 1960s and, meeting with Stroud Cornock, I worked with him on an interactive artwork called *Datapack*, which was shown in the CG70 exhibition at Brunel University in 1970. This was a very early computer-based interactive artwork.

At the same time, we realised that we needed a conceptual framework for talking and thinking about such artworks. We presented a classification of interactive art systems, which we called "the matrix", at the CG70 conference (Cornock and Edmonds, 1970). We identified four situations, which we termed "Static", "Dynamic-Passive", "Dynamic-Interactive", and "Dynamic-Interactive (Varying)". Briefly, "Static" applied to works that do not change, "Dynamic-Passive" to works that changed but were not influenced by the audience, "Dynamic-Interactive" to works that changed as a result of audience actions, and "Dynamic-Interactive (Varying)" applied to interactive works that were also influenced by other factors, so that their response varied. This was the initial framework that I worked with, both in my art and in my HCI research. As we will see, it did not cover all the cases that have turned out to be interesting in my practice, but it did provide a robust starting point.

A useful explanation of Cornock and Edmonds' framework was described as follows.

> "**Static:** The art object does not change and is viewed by a person. There is no interaction between the two that can be observed by someone else, although the viewer may be experiencing personal psychological or emotional reactions. The artwork itself does not respond to its context. This is familiar ground in art galleries and museums where art consumers look at a painting or print, listen to tape recordings and talk to one another about the art on the walls and, generally speaking, obey the command not to touch.
>
> **Dynamic-Passive:** The art object has an internal mechanism that enables it to change or it may be modified by an environmental factor such as temperature, sound or light. The internal mechanism is specified by the artist and any changes that take place are entirely predictable. Sculptures, such as George Rickey's kinetic pieces, that move according to internal mechanisms and also in response to atmospheric changes in the environment fall into this category. The viewer is a passive observer of this activity performed by the artwork in response to the physical environment.
>
> **Dynamic-Interactive:** All of the conditions of the dynamic passive category apply with the added factor that the human "viewer" has an active role in influencing the changes in the art object. For example, by walking over a mat that contains sensors attached to lights operating in variable sequences, the viewer becomes a participant that influences the process of the work. Motion and sound capture techniques can be used to incorporate human activity into the way visual images and sounds are presented. The work "performs" differently according to what the person does or says. There may be more than one participant and more than one art object. An example of this work is the *Iamascope*, a work that includes a camera looking at the viewers and is connected to a controlling computer. The work reacts to human movement in front of it by changing a kaleidoscope-like image and making music at the same time in direct response to the viewer's movements.

Dynamic-Interactive (Varying): The conditions for Dynamic-Interactive apply, with the addition of a modifying agent that changes the original specification of the art object. The agent could be a human or it could be a software program. Because of this, the process that takes place, or rather, the performance of the art system, cannot be predictable. It will depend on the history of interactions with the work. In this case, either the artist from time to time updates the specification of the art object or a software agent that is learning from the experiences of interaction automatically modifies the specification. In this case, the performance of the art object varies, in addition to case 3, according to the history of its experiences" (Candy and Edmonds, 2002a).

#Datapack was of the third kind, Dynamic-Interactive (Figure 4.1).

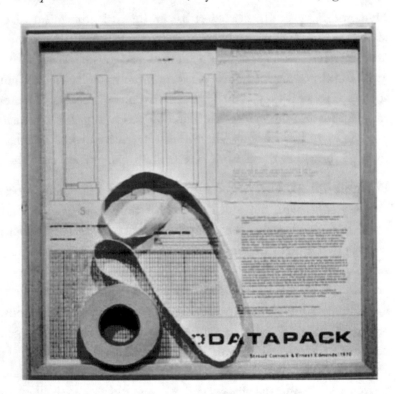

Figure 4.1: Archive material—Cornock and Edmonds *Datapack, 1970.

By modern standards it was technologically very clumsy (this was a decade before the advent of the PC). However, it demonstrated the point. The participant sat at a "teletype" (keyboard and printer combined) and entered into a "conversation" with the computer. This conversation was rather like the famous *Eliza* software (Weizenbaum, 1966) that spotted keywords and used various tricks to respond in ways that could be seen to be plausibly "intelligent". For example, when someone typed in "I feel sad," *Eliza* might respond with "Why do you feel sad?" As in our case, Eliza had no smart intelligent system that understood the user's remarks but rather presented a simulation of conversation that often sounded plausible.

As a result of the conversation, the computer software made certain decisions that determined what graphical output would result. This was in the form of a drawing executed on a plotter. The drawing identified a notional space around the Vickers Building next to the Tate Gallery (now the Tate Britain) in London. A package, including the drawing and a printed copy of the conversation (as produced by the teletype), was then handed to the participant as their artefact to take away. The key issue at this time was to find a way to explore interaction at all. The technical limitations made it difficult to match the theoretical goals, but *Datapack* certainly was interactive and informal discussions with participants at the exhibition indicated that it was also engaging.

4.2   INTERACTION: FROM COMPLEX TO SIMPLE

Working with the relative complexities of *#Datapack* I wondered if it would be possible to make a very simple work that encompassed the same principles. I came up with *JigSaw* (Figure 4.2), which was just 16 wooden pieces that could be fitted together, rather in the manner of a jigsaw puzzle. They were so designed that there were hundreds of different ways of putting them together but each way was highly constrained. The participant could interact with the work by arranging or re-arranging it but its internal logic constrained the result. This work did not quite fit the Cornock and Edmonds framework because that framework was made in order to address computer-based interaction. *JigSaw* was "re-arrangable", however, and I will return to its classification later in the chapter.

Having worked on an interactive and a "re-arrangeable" artwork, I started to explore the nature of interaction itself. I began to ask myself questions like: What is going on when a human interacts with the world around them? What motivates or limits those interactions? This led me to read about various psychological studies of human interaction with the world and with other humans.

Figure 4.2: Edmonds, *Jigsaw*, rearrangeable artwork, wood, 1970.

Current scientific studies of very young infants provided the motive that led to my next development. It seemed that right from birth a child interacts with its environment in a purposeful way: not just to obtain food and so on but also to try to construct understandings about that world. "If I do this and that, will the world do some particular thing?" This very early and basic form of interaction is conducted without a shared language, just by prodding the world and looking at what happens: trying to find patterns (Bower, 1974). Even without reading the scientific literature we can see, just by looking at babies, that they reach out, look and listen in an exploratory way. As one person suggested to me, we can see the scientist in the crib. New things interest them and they do manage to communicate at least to those who care for them.

As a result of my reading about early infant behaviour I started to think about ways in which I might deal with such issues in an artwork. I did not want to build an imitation of an infant, but I tried to think of what might be essential elements of their situation in relation to interaction. I thought about interacting with the world in restricted ways and without language. I thought about ways in which I might make interactive art that explored such situations. As a result, I started building what I came to call my *Communication Game* series of works (Figures 4.3 and 4.4). These interactive works were concerned with humans interacting with humans through technology (rather than humans interacting with technology). In part, they represented a realisation of Ascott's "telematic art" in that they transformed the viewer into an active participant in creating the artwork (Edmonds, 1975). The intentions were to restrict communication between participant to a very low bandwidth, to provide no instructions or code and to add a certain amount of complexity. The complexity was injected by having what a participant saw controlled by two other participants, only one of whom saw the results of that participant's actions. We could say that the data that a participant was working with was incomplete or noisy, as tends to be the case in all normal life situations.

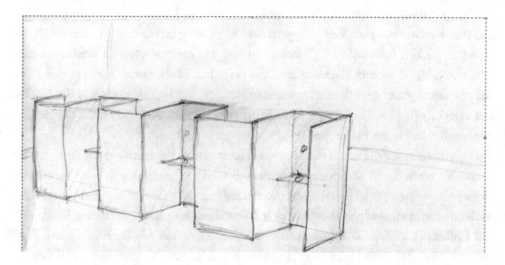

Figure 4.3: Drawing of *Communication Game 1*, Ernest Edmonds. Leicester Polytechnic, 1970.

Figure 4.4: *Communication Game* as constructed and shown at De Montfort University, Leicester, 2017.

After a few iterations of the *Communication Games* work, including the use of sound, I left it alone until about 2006, when I re-started the development of that series in the form of the *Cities Tango* artworks, of which more later on.

In my own art practice, I left interaction alone for some years. I was still interested, but I was not content with any of the technological methods that I found. And so I put significant effort into HCI research. However, I worked with Ph.D. students and other artists on a number of approaches to making interactive art. Steve Bell, for example, looked in detail at different strategies. He concentrated on work that used a "life" model of growth and restricted the participant's actions to very specific roles, such as seeding the growth of a dynamic work (Bell, 1991). This work was time-based and certainly involved interaction, but the interaction was essentially quite simple. The complexity was more in the growth of the image over time.

Mike Quantrill is a different case. He explored interactive drawing using an electronic whiteboard and made experimental works in which participant movement (detected by floor pads) determined the nature and dynamics of a visual display. The audience could almost play the work as if it was an audio-visual instrument (Edmonds and Quantrill, 1998). So in Quantrill's case the interaction was continuous and fluid. Growth was the central interest in Bell's work and interaction was the central interest in Quantrill's. Both of them have continued to explore these interests.

At the time when I was not directly working with interaction in art (1980s and 1990s), rather, I was concentrating on another implication of computation for art. That was generative time-based artwork, in which a set of rules that I designed led to the unfolding of an abstract work over a period of time, sometimes extending to hours or days (Edmonds, 2003). By 2001, however, I had seen how to incorporate interaction into my time-based generative works. The addition of interaction to the generative works represented a particular example of the category discussed above, Dynamic-Interactive (Varying). In this case, the variation came from the internal generative system. The interaction came, for example, from the analysis of images of the audience captured by a camera, typically a small webcam. Other forms of input used were sound and pressure on floor pads.

The generative process in these works is dynamic in itself but what I added was an input to the art system that could cause a change in that dynamic process. The typical mechanism was to have the process consult data from the camera as part of the determination of the next action. Thus, activities external to the artwork itself, such as audience behaviour, altered the generative process. I often used image processing, taking data from a video camera pointing at the audience and analyzing movement or sound analysis of voice. To begin with, I made works in which the alteration was direct and immediately visible: audience actions caused visible responses. One example using floor pads was *Absolute 4.6*, which was made in collaboration with Mark Fell. A back-projected wall screen displayed vertical colour stripes and a sound system generated related abstract noise. The floor pads covered an area in front of the screen and the system's behaviour was modified both in terms of the pace of change and the colours and sounds used as people moved towards the screen or to the right or left. The general nature of change was consistent but the particular colours and sounds varied over time in relation to audience location (Edmonds, 2006).

4.3   INTERACTION: FROM REACTION TO INFLUENCE

The psychological underpinning of interaction, as it is mostly employed in HCI as well as in art, is the study of action and response. In this view, each action (input to the system) leads to a response (by the system) that, in turn, encourages or enables another action. This view of interaction is oversimplified. It does not take long-term influence properly into account. Put simply, the key issue is that a system as complex as a human must have internal states that represent memory, mood, state of development, etc. An interaction, be it with another human, an artwork, or a computer, can influence internal states. This can happen whether or not any immediate action is made. Hence, at times no response to an input may be made although an internal change may have occurred. Engagement over long periods of time almost certainly involves changes in these internal states and so an interactive artwork that is successful in these terms must take this into account.

The psychological models most interesting for interactive art, and I suggest for HCI, are not action response ones but Systems Theory ones (Edmonds, 2007a). The action response models deal with immediate reactions to events. In a mechanical system where when we pull a lever, for example, various physical connections directly lead to a door opening without delay: the response. In Systems Theory the interchanges between interlinked parts are viewed in a much broader context. Most significantly, the system is taken to have an internal state that is partly used to determine behaviour. For example, my mood (an internal state) might be happy or sad. Someone complains about something I said (an action) and it might change me from happy to sad but I might not say or do anything at that moment (no response). Later in the day I might sit and watch TV rather than go to a party, which I would have done if I had felt happy. For interactive art, this perspective introduces the possibility of considering interactions that have effects in the future and that may have no observable response at the time.

A simple art example would be where an art system has a memory of audience actions that is only used to affect the artworks behaviour days or weeks later. I have suggested elsewhere that "influence" might be a better term than "interaction" to describe such cases (Edmonds, 2007a). The idea behind this is that audience actions influence the behaviour of the art system without their necessarily being an obvious interaction. A consequence that appeals to me is that we can then talk about it the other way round, where the art system influences the audience. Naturally, this is one thing that an artist might hope for.

4.4   LONG-TERM ENGAGEMENT

I started to explore the idea of moving from interaction to influence in 2003. This work matured in a series begun in 2007, called *Shaping Form*; see Figure 4.5. Images are generated using rules that determine the colours, patterns, and timing (Edmonds, 2007b). These are generative works that are changed by the influence of the environment around them. Movement in front of each work is detected by image analysis and leads to continual changes in the program that generates the images. People can readily detect the immediate responses of the work to movement but the changes over time are only apparent when there is more prolonged, although not necessarily continuous, contact with it. A first viewing followed by one several months later will reveal noticeable changes in the colours and patterns. The *Shaping Form* series are the latest works arising from my preoccupation with interaction and time expressed in a wide range of abstract generative forms over many years.

Digital artworks like *Shaping Form* are designed to interact with the environment in which they are found. Exactly how they behave depends on what kind of compositional elements or principles are being worked with at the time. I work with structural relationships between visual elements, the colours, and shapes, which determine how the images are constructed. Some works are made to learn from external movement such as a hand waving or a person walking by. The way the art systems accumulate information from these inputs, or "learns", determines how they select future choices of colour and pattern in the images displayed. The behaviour of the works is not intended to always be obvious, so that if you continuously try to force a response by waving, it might result in a period of quiet. Each *Shaping Form* has a generative element, a computer program, which produces a continuous stream of images using predefined rules that control the rectangular pattern, the pallet of colours and the timing. The program continuously analyses movements detected in front of the work. As a result of this analysis, the rules are steadily modified in a way that accumulates a history of experiences over the life of the work. For example, long quiet periods might lead to the colours becoming brighter and the action faster. The shaping of the form is a never-ending process of development.

Figure 4.5: *Shaping Form* works in an exhibition, 2007.

4.5   DISTRIBUTED INTERACTION

My earlier concern for communication through digital systems, exemplified in the *Communication Game* works, continued, for example by making a version of *Shaping Form* that worked on the World Wide Web. This changed the structure to include a shared memory and the possibility of many remote users and so united the core ideas of *Shaping Form* with *Communication Game*. The main step, however, came about between 2008 and 2009 with the development of the *Cities Tango* series (Figures 4.6 and 4.7) (Edmonds, 2009). Ascott's early concept of Telematic Art that advocates the use of computer-mediated networks as an art medium is similar (Ascott, 1966).

In *Cities Tango*, there are two or more separate parts of the art system. Each one consists of a *Shaping Form* like piece with camera input. The parts are connected over the Internet. The first major example had one part in Sydney and a second in Belfast. In addition to the typical colour bands that I use, I added two other elements. First I used photographs of a single location at each site at different times of the day as abstract elements that substituted for certain colours and gave a sense of the remote site. Second, occasional live stills were transmitted from one site to another, typically at a time of significant audience activity. Thus we have the idea of distributed interactive art systems that can involve instant response and/or communication as well as long-term influence in the *Shaping Form* sense.

Figure 4.6: *Cities Tango*, Belfast and Sydney, in Sydney 2009

4.6   INTERACTION ENGAGEMENT AND EXPERIENCE

The direct physical way in which the audience interacts with a work is a major part of any art system. Three main approaches are used. The first is as in *#Datapack*, where members of the audience physically manipulate the work in some way (typing at the teletype in *#Datapack*). In this case the participant directly acts upon the art system. The second approach is where members of the audience are provided with special devices of some kind, such as headsets as in Char Davies' works using virtual reality (McRobert, 2007) or biological sensors as in *Cardiomorphologies* (Khut and Muller, 2005). Here, a human facilitator helps the participant by equipping them with, for example, a headset. The third approach is ambient, such as many of the examples described in this book, where audience movements, or states, are detected by non-invasive devices, such as cameras, floor pads, or infrared beams. In this case, there is no physical contact between the participant and the art system and no human helper.

Figure 4.7: *Cities Tango*, Belfast and Sydney, in Belfast 2009

We can term these approaches:

• Direct

• Facilitated

• Ambient

Issues about the audience reaction to Dynamic-Interactive works are significant and have gained increasing attention. These issues are largely concerned with engagement, as I have noted, and include engagement at a distance and over time.

In my own practice, I have just considered three kinds of engagement that I will discuss in Section 5.3. Let's call them:

• Attracting

• Sustaining

• Relating

Attracting is a matter of drawing attention, e.g., a sudden noise (or a sudden silence) will attract attention. Sustaining is the process of retaining that attention for a period of time. Relating is developing a long-term interest, which occurs when the audience wants to experience the work again and again, perhaps over many years. Attracting and relating do not always go together. Sometimes, what is most immediately engaging is also easily discarded. My *Shaping Form* works, for example, clearly aim at a Relating type of engagement. The challenge is to provide just enough attracting and sustaining engagement to draw the audience in, but no so much as to induce boredom.

4.7   CATEGORIES OF INTERACTION REVISITED

I have discussed three kinds of classification in relation to interactive art. The first was the one that dealt with the kind of interactive system being used: the Cornock and Edmonds framework. The second was of the different kinds of way that the physical exchange takes place. The third was the set of different kind of experience that the interaction encourages in the audience.

The systems categories that I described in Section 4.1 extended the early Cornock and Edmonds terminology. To make the naming more consistent, we can replace "Dynamic-Interactive" by "Dynamic-Interactive (Responding)". This implies that the system responds directly to audience action, at the time of that action, and so is directly reactive. In addition, it seems helpful to add the Rearrangeable category that includes, for example, Johnson's "The Unfortunates" mentioned above. I use the term "open", following Eco (1962), meaning that the work is, in a sense, unfinished. There are decisions that can be made and alternative forms that can be selected to complete a definitive instance of the work.

Thus we now have:

- Static

- Dynamic-Passive

- Dynamic-Interactive:

    ○ Open

    ○ Responding

    ○ Varying

    ○ Influencing

    ○ Communicating

The core interest in relation to interactive art in this chapter, and in the book, is in the dynamic-interactive cases, so we might simplify our categories by saying that we have five kinds of interactive art *systems*:

- Open

- Responding

- Varying

- Influencing

- Communicating

Of course, art systems may fall into more than one of these categories. For example, the *Shaping Form* works are both Varying and Influencing. The *Communication Games* are both Responding and Communicating. All four categories apply to *Cities Tango*.

As discussed above, the *physical* interactions might be any of:

- Direct

- Facilitated

- Ambient

Each kind of system might be implemented with various physical interfaces. However, we can see that the Influencing case, for example, may not be easily realised by the Facilitated method, for the simple reason that it may not be practical to facilitate over long periods of time.

In relation to experience, I have discussed:

• Attracting

• Sustaining

• Relating

I have described three dimensions in which to consider interactive art systems, each of which are found in HCI: system, physical, and experience.

4.8   REVISITING THE EXAMPLE ARTWORKS

Having discussed and established these dimensions, I will revisit the examples of my work mentioned above and discuss each of them in terms of those dimensions. This gives concrete examples of the various categories.

#Datapack

This work was purely a Responding art system. A single participant typed at a keyboard and the machine responded directly, asking a series of questions. Once the conversation was complete, the plot was drawn and the participant was handed their personal pack. The physical interaction at the teletype was direct. The participant pushed keys. However, the whole process was Facilitated by a human helper, first in helping a participant operate the teletype[9] and then in operating the plotter and putting the pack together. In terms of the intended experience, perhaps the main concern was to provide sufficient interest to encourage a participant in Sustaining interest through the process. There was no expectation that people would particularly come back and try it again, although there was a hope that the pack would be intriguing enough to have some longer-term interest.

---

[9] Although the teletype has gone, it was almost us unfamiliar to the public in 1970 as it is now. In fact, the idea of the general public directly working with a computer was novel in those days.

Jigsaw

Jigsaw is not interactive in an explicit way. However, it could be re-arranged, by physical action, within constraints that were integral properties of the shapes themselves. It is, therefore, an interactive work in that it required or encouraged the participation of the audience in completing the work. *Jigsaw* is Open. Interaction with it is direct and it emphasises Sustaining engagement and, I hope, Relating engagement.

Communication Game

The various versions of this work were all Communicating art systems. *Communication Game* is not a responding system because, should there only be one participant, no responses occur at all. Everything that a participant sees or hears (there were several versions based on lights and one based on sound output) came about as a result of other participant actions. The physical interactions were Direct, the flicking of switches without any facilitation or instruction being provided. The work was Attracting in so far as available switches in a public space tend to invite action, but in no other sense unless seeing others interacting raised interest. The Sustaining element came from the fact that, whilst participants typically felt as if they were controlling something the responses were not consistent, depending as they did on the behaviour of others. This tension between feeling in control and not being able to predict seems to be a significant factor in achieving a Sustaining experience.

Shaping Form

The core of these works includes a time-based generative system together with an image analysis system that slowly modifies the generative rules governing, hue, saturation, brightness, stripe patterns and timing. The image analysis primarily generates internal information about the amount of movement in front of the work at any one time. The *Shaping Form* works are Influencing art systems. The actions taken by the audience influence the behaviour and appearance of the work in an accumulating way over long periods of time. In order to give some indication to the audience that the work is interacting there is a "fast response" component that works in a Responding mode. When movement above a particular threshold is detected a clear immediate visual change is made that signals recognition of the movement. The physical interaction with a *Shaping Form* is purely Ambient, relying as it does on image analysis. The intended experience is one of the audience *relating* to the work, most probably through living with it or seeing it regularly in an often visited space. The fast response provides an attracting quality. However, it has proved difficult to judge the correct balance between the Influencing and the Responding behaviours. If the response is too frequent and easily achieved it seems to dominate the experience. Later *Shaping Forms* have, therefore, reduced the fast response activity. The Sustaining element of these works is not intended to come through interaction at all, but relies on intrinsic aesthetic interest.

Cities Tango

This series of works brings the concept of *Communication Game* together with that of *Shaping Form*. In effect, two shaping form-like elements are located in different cities (e.g., Belfast and Sydney) and connected together via the Internet through a shared server. In *Cities Tango*, the movement analysis, taking place at one location, is used to influence the generative behaviour at the other. Hence, the work is essentially a Communicating art system. To make the link more concrete, a set of images at each location (taken from the same spot at different times of the day) is used in an abstract way to replace one of the colours in the generative system. Hence, the displayed stripes include, from time to time, images of the remote city. The work is, however, also Responding in a more significant sense than in the *Shaping Form* pieces. When movement is sufficient to trigger a fast response, the latest image from the remote camera is displayed for a few seconds. Thus, activity at one location reveals a real-time image from the other. The Responding element of *Cities Tango* is more central to the work than in *Shaping Form* and the dilemma of balance with the Influencing element is therefore not problematic. In fact, the Influencing element only becomes important when the work is in place over a long period, which has not been the case at the time of writing. As with *Shaping Form* the interaction is Ambient. However, the experiences that are facilitated are more general. The work is Attracting in the sense that a dynamic display including images from afar is shown. It is Sustaining in part by nature of the revealing of the real time images that often include pictures of participants in the other city. The intention is that it is Relating because of the developing and changing nature of what is seen.

4.9   ON THE IMPLICATIONS FOR HCI

Over the long period of working with computers, making art and evolving my approach I have learnt many lessons that have been applied to HCI. As I mentioned near the start of this chapter, a number of them have been described in Francesca Franco's book (2018). Some of these lessons are still important to stress and learn from. In this chapter, I argue that the basic nature of the interactive system can be described in terms of the different relationships between people and systems as used in the art domain and clearly, we can categorise the different physical forms of interaction identified. Most importantly, we can categorise different forms of interactive experience using the results of the developments in art practice and I will describe more such results in the next chapter. All these results lead to different design criteria and different evaluation possibilities and each one is a topic for research.

I have explained the limitations of the action-response model for describing interaction and proposed the term "Influence"—interactions that have effects over long periods of time—as a better descriptor. The point is that we need better research methods and more attention to understanding Influence. In a distributed, connected, interactive world, finding how best to engage and facilitate human creativity is a major goal of HCI. Art can help!

One valuable contribution that art can make is in its practice-based research methods. They are very relevant to HCI. For example, they place the artefact as a central element in the research process and offer documented reflection as a valuable method. Of course, there is much more and I will point to some other lessons as I go through the case studies in the next chapter.

Interactive art systems involve artefacts and audiences equally. The artist sets up situations that develop in ways that are, at least in part, determined by the audience. The cybernetic and systems principles that informed the early developments are now applied, more completely than at first, by the equal and reflexive consideration of art object and active audience experience. As a result, the frameworks that inform our thinking and practice have had to evolve appropriately. There is no question that they will evolve still further as new opportunities, new understandings, and new practices emerge.

CHAPTER 5

Case Studies and Lessons

In this chapter I present examples of art research that are significant from an HCI perspective, pointing out some of the main lessons that can be learnt.

5.1   ART, GAMES, AND PLAY

The computer game arose from the technological opportunities that have emerged. In fact, computer games and interactive art often have much in common. In this case study I report some interesting work about play, art, and games. The concern, however, is not directly about play and games as such. Rather, it is an investigation, in the context of art, about a language in the form of a set of named categories that enables us to talk about and think about the nature of play in interactive systems.

The intention in a game can be quite different to the intention in an artwork, but both may involve the audience/player/user in intense interaction with a computer-controlled device (call it artwork or game) that is driven by some form of play, pleasure or curiosity. The human, confronted with the system, takes an action that the work responds to. Typically, a sequence of actions and responses develop and continue until a goal is reached or the human is satisfied or bored. The nature of play can be the subject of an artist's work and this is no problem for the artist. Back in the year 2000, however, it was still a problem for curators. In the UK's Millennium Dome all of the interactive art was shown in the Play Zone and none of it was included in the list of artworks on show. Exhibiting interactive art is still somewhat problematic, but the issues that the artist faces go beyond that because their practice has to change in order to deal with interaction.

In the context of making interactive art, Brigid Costello has argued that the nature of play can best be understood through taxonomy that she has termed a "pleasure framework" (Costello, 2007). She has synthesized a collection of research results relating to pleasure into 13 categories. It is important to note that pleasure takes many forms, some of which can be quite challenging and may not be "nice" or "delightful." Costello describes the categories as follows.

> "*Creation* is the pleasure participants get from having the power to create something while interacting with a work. It is also the pleasure participants get from being able to express themselves creatively.

Exploration is the pleasure participants get from exploring a situation. Exploration is often linked with the next pleasure, discovery, but not always. Sometimes it is fun to just explore.

Discovery is the pleasure participants get from making a discovery or working something out.

Difficulty is the pleasure participants get from having to develop a skill or to exercise skill in order to do something. Difficulty might also occur at an intellectual level in works that require a certain amount of skill to understand them or an aspect of their content.

Competition is the pleasure participants get from trying to achieve a defined goal. This could be a goal that is defined by them or it might be one that is defined by the work. Completing the goal could involve working with or against another human participant, a perceived entity within the work, or the system of the work itself.

Danger is the pleasure of participants feeling scared, in danger, or as if they are taking a risk. This feeling might be as mild as a sense of unease or might involve a strong feeling of fear.

Captivation is the pleasure of participants feeling mesmerized or spellbound by something or of feeling like another entity has control over them.

Sensation is the pleasure participants get from the feeling of any physical action the work evokes, e.g., touch, body movements, hearing, vocalizing etc.

Sympathy is the pleasure of sharing emotional or physical feelings with something.

Simulation is the pleasure of perceiving a copy or representation of something from real life.

Fantasy is the pleasure of perceiving a fantastical creation of the imagination.

Camaraderie is the pleasure of developing a sense of friendship, fellowship or intimacy with someone.

Subversion is the pleasure of breaking rules or of seeing others break them. It is also the pleasure of subverting or twisting the meaning of something or of seeing someone else do so."

This categorization is drawn from a wide collection of studies. The way in which the various theories contributed to this framework is summarized in Table 5.1. For more details, see Costello and Edmonds's paper (Costello and Edmonds, 2007). The source material as published by the various researchers (Caillois, 1962; Groos, 1901; Csikszentmihalyi, 1975; Apter, 1991; Garneau, 2001; Hunicke et al., 2004; Berlyne, 1968).

Table 5.1: Costello's summary of theories that contributed to her pleasure framework

Groos	Callois	Csikszent	Apter	Garneau	LeBlanc	Framework
Pleasure of Being a Cause				Power Creation	Expression	Creation
			Exploration			Exploration
				Discovery	Discovery	Discovery
		Problem Solving		Intellectual Problem Solving		
			Challenge	Application of Skill	Challenge	Difficulty
	Competition	Competition		Competition Advancement & Completion		Competition
	Chance	Risk & Chance	Facing Danger	Thrill of Danger		Danger
				Immersion Beauty	Submission	Captivation
	Vertigo		Arousing Stimulation	Physical Activity	Sensation	Sensation
Aesthetic Sympathy						Sympathy
Pleasure of Make Believe	Simulation	Creative	Fiction & Narrative		Narrative	Simulation
					Fantasy	Fantasy
		Friendship & Relaxation		Love Social Interaction	Fellowship	Camaraderie
			Negativism Cognition Synergy	Comedy		Subversion

Each of the categories of pleasure represents a form of interaction with its own characteristics. Each has to be considered in its own way, providing a context in which appropriate interaction design decisions can be made. In Costello's work, the framework has been applied in the design and development of interactive artworks. For her, play and pleasure formed the goals of the artwork or, at least, the nature of the interactive experience being addressed (Costello, 2009).

The subject of the art in such cases is play and pleasure and the works engage the audience in playful behaviours. The aesthetic results, of course, may be important in other respects. Art is multi-layered and we certainly must not assume that the significance of playful art is limited to play itself. In games, on the other hand, the top level of interest may represent the "point" of the system. Even then, however, other layers may add depth to the experience. The boundaries between games and art can be very grey and, for the purposes of this book, it may be assumed that the complete art/game gamut is often best seen as one.

5.1.1   LESSONS

- We use broad terms to describe experiences but need to break them down as is done here with "pleasure" and "play." In HCI design, it is important to be very clear about the kind of experience that a user might experience and that the designer hopes to facilitate. Terms such as "pleasure" or "engagement" are too general, covering too many different cases. Each more specific form of play, for example, will lead to its own design and evaluation criteria.

- Costello's framework is directly applicable to HCI. The framework is outlined above but described more fully in the referenced paper. It can be used directly in HCI to form specific design criteria, such as the user should experience a feeling of mild danger.

- Each category is a topic for research. The categories can be used to frame specific research questions, such as what are the features of an interactive experience that encourage the perception of involvement in fantasy?

5.2   ART, BETA-TESTING, AND EXPERIENCE DESIGN

In this case study, I will consider the process of making interactive art. In particular, I describe one way that has been adopted to help the artist understand the interactive characteristics of their artwork.

As I have discussed earlier in this book, a painter might not explicitly consider the viewer at all. It is quite possible to paint a picture by only considering the properties of the paint, the colours and the forms constructed with them. In an interactive work, on the other hand, as behaviour is central to its very existence, the artist can hardly ignore audience engagement within the making process. This is where the most significant implications of interactive art for creative practice lie. As we know from the world of HCI, reliable predictions of human behaviour in relation to interactive systems are not available, only in certain very simple cases. Observation, in some sense, of an interactive system in action is the only way to understand it. Consider, for example, the issues identified in Costello's categories described in case study one. To use them an artist has to find ways of incorporating observation of some kind into practice. This is an extension of the role of research in practice.

We have seen that a significant feature of the increasing role of research has been the need for artists to try their works out with the public before completion. Because an interactive work is not complete without participants and because the nature of the interactive experience may depend significantly on context, an artist cannot finish the work alone in the studio. This can be seen as a problem in that showing a half-finished work may be quite unattractive to the creator; on the face of it, there seems to be no easy way out of the situation.

Figure 5.1: *Beta_Space* in Powerhouse Museum, Sydney.

An example of an approach to solving this problem is *Beta_Space*. The Powerhouse Museum Sydney and the Creativity and Cognition Studios, University of Technology, Sydney collaborated to create *Beta_Space*, an experimental exhibition environment where the public can engage with the latest research in art and technology. It ran for about ten years in the early part of this century and showed interactive artworks in development that were ready for some kind of evaluation and/or refinement in response to participant engagement.

The works shown were at different stages, from early prototype to final product. In all cases engagement with the public provided critical information for further iterations of the artwork or of the research (Edmonds et al., 2009). Evaluation methods drawn in various ways from HCI were employed to provide the artist with a valuable understanding of their work in action. There are a number of different perspectives that need to be taken into account, including artist, curator, and researcher (Muller et al., 2006). It was explained in that paper as follows.

"The *artist* is concerned with the artwork itself and its functioning within the art system. The central issues are to do with making the work or defining the system within which it operates. The artists' questions are variations of "How should I make this aspect of the artwork?" The *curator* is primarily concerned with facilitating the encounter between the artwork and the audience. This includes supporting both the artist's and the audience's process of making and perceiving the work. The *evaluator* looks at the behaviour of the system in its context in order to understand important aspects of human behaviour.

When the evaluator role is combined with one of the others, the viewpoint taken is one that serves the specific practical goals associated with the other role. When the evaluation viewpoint stands alone it tries to be more generic and to understand better, for example, the cognitive processes that the audiences become involved in.

The artist's viewpoint is one that focuses on issues that influence practical decisions about how the work is made or modified in order to successfully realise the vision or intention. The artwork is the focus of concern. Exhibitions are important to artists but are often not the central issue.

The role of the contemporary curator has evolved beyond its origins as a keeper and carer of objects, towards a more dynamic and proactive position as a facilitator of situations and a mediator between artists, artworks and audiences. Interactive art requires that curators find ways to investigate and work with the experiences of the audience and to find ways of helping the artist work with the material of experience.

The evaluator's viewpoint is one that tries to gain knowledge and understanding of the audience experience that is as reliable as possible. One of the challenging questions in this view is whether it is possible to identify and measure engagement with interactive art as audiences experience it in a gallery/museum environment."

The key step has been to incorporate HCI research into the interactive art making process. But what is the contribution to HCI?

First, the idea of *Beta_Space* itself is not that unfamiliar in HCI. It is a case of "evaluation in the wild", where the context is real rather than in a possibly misleading laboratory context. For the artist, a public exhibition space will often be perfect, but we have to translate that to whatever is most appropriate for the interactive system being evaluated. So spaces "in the wild" where designs can be tried out as if they were real and delivered are crucially important.

Second, the evaluation methods have to be unobtrusive. In the case of Beta_ Space, the main method was video-cued recall. This was explained in the above-mentioned paper as follows.

> "This method for collecting verbal data is commonly used for investigating human cognitive processes. Because reports are made after the experience, this method is regarded as having less impact on the experience than the think-aloud method (Ericsson and Simon, 1993). Reporting retrospectively, however, presents the risk that the participant will forget details and that their recall will be filtered. The video-cued recall method helps to avoid these pitfalls by using video to help the participant recall the detail of their experience and avoid selective recounting. Suchman (1987) argues that verbal data obtained using video records can more accurately reflect lived experience than verbal data from interviews.
>
> Her argument is backed up by results from recent studies using video-cued recall methods, such as Bentley et al., (2003). These studies reveal that not only does this method enable participants to recall more detail about their experience but also more importantly to recall preverbal perceptual, motivational and affective states that rarely emerge from interview data" (Muller et al., 2006).

The third point is to translate the names of the three roles. I think that is quite easy. Moving from art to design, the artist becomes the designer, the curator becomes the supplier and the evaluator, of course, remains just that.

5.2.1 LESSONS

- Beta testing "in the wild" is common in HCI, but this work illustrates how engagement with public delivery platforms can support it. Many HCI studies were conducted in usability laboratories, but we need to take that approach into the street, the office, the classroom, the bus, and the bar in order to beta test HCI embodied in real contexts.

- There are different stakeholders in any interactive system and the evaluation methods needed in relation to each may be quite different. In any one example of interaction, there may be many stakeholders. There is often more than one user directly experiencing the system at any one time. Then there may be information providers or receivers, people monitoring the process (technically, managerially, or from a security perspective), etc. The user experience has to be measured from all of these perspectives and the evaluation methods used will be different in each case.

- The multiple viewpoint issue is a topic for research—in the wild. How to conduct HCI research covering multiple stakeholders, with the need for multiple methods, is a research question in itself. Conducting it "in the wild" and gathering multiple accounts of experience, as we need to do, is even more challenging.

5.3 ART, ENGAGEMENT, AND RESEARCH

In this study we see HCI methods used to enhance art research and new approaches developed which can feed back into HCI. As I have stressed from the start of this book, an important area in interactive art practice is the design of the interactive experience itself. So, as we have seen, HCI methods contribute to interactive art making. From HCI we know how a designer can shape software in ways that make it easy to use but that shaping may be a mystery to others. It is an issue of distinguishing between the models of the system held by the various players: programmer, designer, and user (Norman, 1988).

Confusion often happens when the designer makes an unconscious assumption that is not shared by others. For example, when an item is dragged over and "dropped" on a waste bin icon, it will normally be made ready to be deleted but retained for the moment. People new to computers sometimes assume that it is lost forever and so are nervous about using it, leading to behaviours that may be unexpected by the designer. The same kind of thing can happen with interactive art. The artist may or may not mind, but they do need to be aware of such issues and make conscious decisions about them.

A growth area in HCI research is Experience Design, as discussed, for example, by Shedroff (2001). This is particularly important because it represents a collection of methods and approaches that concentrate on understanding the audience-participant-user experience. It does not emphasise the interface, as the early HCI work used to do, but looks at human experience and how the design of the behaviour of the system influences it.

One specific common area of interest between interactive art and experience design is engagement. Do people become engaged with the artwork? Is that engagement sustained? What are the factors that influence the nature of the engagement? Does engagement relate to pleasure, frustration, challenge, or anger, for example? Of course, the artist can use himself or herself as subject and rely on their own reactions to guide their work. Much art is made like that, although asking the opinion of expert peers, at least, is also normal. However, understanding audience engagement with interactive works is quite a challenge and needs more extensive investigation than introspection, and that is where this study was directed.

Zafer Bilda developed a model of the engagement process in relation to audience studies with a range of artworks in Beta_Space (Bilda et al., 2008). The process is illustrated in Figure 5.2.

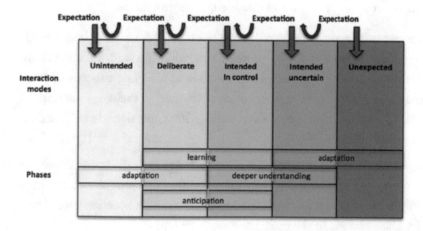

Figure 5.2: Model of engagement: Interaction modes and phases over time.

Note that the engagement mode shifts over time from audience interaction from unintended actions through deliberate ones that can lead to a sense of control.

In some works it moves on into modes with more exploration and uncertainty. Four interaction phases were identified: adaptation, learning, anticipation, and deeper understanding.

Adaptation: Participants adapt to the changes in the environment; learning how to behave and how to set expectations, working with uncertainty. This phase often occurs from unintended mode through to deliberate mode. The participant may return to this phase later on, when they are able to make deliberate, controlled actions that lead to adaptation: a mode that can go on to be disrupted by unexpected events.

Learning: Participants start developing and an internal/mental model of what the system does, this also means that they develop (and change) expectations, emotions, and behaviours, accessing memories and beliefs. In this phase the participant interprets exchanges, explores and experiments relationships between initiation and feedback from the system. Therefore, they develop expectations on how to initiate certain feedback and accumulate interpretations of exchanges. This phase can occur from deliberate mode to intended/in control mode.

Anticipation: In this phase, participants know what the system will do in relation to initiation, in other words they predict the interaction. Intention is more grounded compared to the previous phases. This phase can occur from deliberate to intended/in control mode.

Deeper understanding: Participants reach a more complete understanding of the artwork and what his or her relationship is to the artwork. In this phase participants judge and evaluate at a higher, conceptual level. They may discover a new aspect of an artwork or an exchange not noticed before. This phase can occur from intended/in control mode to intended/ uncertain mode.

Comparing these phases with the pleasure framework discussed above, we can see that the categories may be most likely to be found in different phases. For example, discovery might be common in the learning phase, whilst subversion might be more likely in the later phases. In designing for engagement, the artist needs to consider where they sit in this space and what kind of engagement or engagement process they are concerned with.

There are many forms of engagement that may be desired in an artwork (Edmonds et al., 2006). For example, in museum studies people talk about attractors—

attributes of an exhibit that encourage the public to pay attention and so become engaged. They have "attraction power", in Bollo and Dal Pozzolo's term (Bollo and Dal Pozzolo, 2005). In a busy public place, be it museum or bar, there are many distractions and points of interest. The attractor is some feature of the interactive art system that is inclined to cause passers by to pay attention to the work and at least approach it, look at it or listen for a few moments.

The immediate question arises of how long such engagement might last and we find that the attributes that encourage sustained engagement are not the same as those that attract. Sustainers have holding power and create "hot spots", in Bollo and Dal Pozzolo's term. So, presuming that the attractors have gained attention, it is necessary to start to engage the audience in a way that can sustain interest for a noticeable period of time. This aspect of engagement might typically be found in the learning phase of Bilda's model.

Another form of engagement is one that extends over long periods of time, where one goes back for repeated experiences such as seeing a favorite play in many performances throughout ones life. These Relaters, as discussed above, are factors that enable the hot spot to remain hot on repeated visits to the exhibition. A good set of relaters meet the highest approval in the world of museums and galleries. This aspect of engagement might typically be found in the deeper understanding phase of Bilda's model. We often find that this long-term form of engagement is not associated with a strong initial attraction. Engagement can grow with experience. These issues are ones that the interactive artist needs to be clear about and the choices have significant influence on the nature of the interaction employed. We saw above that Costello, for example, takes a particular (but not exclusive) interest in sustainers of engagement in her art. Another example of developing an artwork around the idea of engagement is in my description of working on a commission for the *White Noise* exhibition (Edmonds, 2006) and my use of the ideas of Section 4.6 above.

Most artists would probably say that they aimed for their work to encourage long-term engagement with their audience. Much interactive art, however, seems to emphasise attraction and immediate engagement. Why is this? One reason is the seductive appeal of direct interaction that has been so powerfully exploited in computer games. However, direct interaction also represents a challenge to the artist taking the long-term view. How is the interactive artwork going to retain its interest once the initial pleasure has worn off? An answer may be implied in another reason for the emphasis on the immediate, which is an emphasis on the action-response model of interaction discussed in the next section.

Artist's aims include a number of issues that are quite generally important, such as the desire for long-term engagement. So, as before, we have some clear lessons for HCI.

5.3.1   LESSONS

- The nature of the engagement with an interactive system changes over time—often in major ways. An HCI system may be used over quite long periods and it is well understood that the nature of the engagement and the way that someone interacts with it can change significantly over time. Evaluation, however, is often done in respect to the experience at just one moment in this cycle and, usually, at a rather early stage. HCI design needs to be done for the life of a system in use, and evaluation methods need to match this need.

- The discussion in case study two, Section 5.2, can usefully be considered in relation to this case. The need is to consider design and perform evaluation about interaction at different times in the life cycle in the wild, in real situations. Imaginative approaches to research design are much needed in order to tackle this problem.

- Design criteria need to be clearly linked to the phases of engagement that are to be addressed. HCI design criteria may well need to be different for different stages in the life cycle and should be identified as early as possible in order to help with the complex design problem posed by this issue.

- Designing interaction to facilitate transitions between phases may be important. In fact, the issue of facilitating transitions as the user's needs, skills, and experiences change is a problem worthy of quite specific HCI research.

- Each phase is a topic for research, as are the transitions. It is useful to take each element of Bilda's model and pose HCI research questions about how its needs can best be met.

5.4   SOCIAL MIXED-REALITY PLAY SPACE

This study described here is of a large mixed-reality artwork in which actors perform. It allows children to explore a landscape and virtual creatures in a social space.

The work was a collaboration between Andrew Bluff and Andrew Johnston (2017a; 2017b). They describe *Creature:Interactions* as follows.

"…a large-scale mixed-reality artwork that incorporates immersive visuals, interactive technology, and live actor facilitation to promote full-body movement and social play. The artwork is set in an animated Australian bush landscape that is magically conjured to life by the full-bodied movements of the participants. Participants interact with a range of native Australian animals including koalas, kangaroos, wombats, birds, and lizards represented as giant line-drawn "totem" creatures (Figure 5.3) and photographic particle clouds that morph and dissolve in response to movement. It features a full 360° interactive visual display that can be presented in 2D or stereoscopic 3D and paired with multichannel audio to create a highly immersive experience that can be enjoyed by audiences of up to 90 people simultaneously. The work transports the audience to a number of Outback locations and simulates environmental events such as bushfires and rainstorms before ascending to the virtual treetops to interact with the moon and night stars.

The work that we created is an interactive companion piece to the *Creature: Dot and the Kangaroo* (Stalker, 2015) physical theater show inspired by Ethel C. Pedley's (2014) classic Australian children's novel in which a little girl, Dot, is lost in the bush and befriends a mother kangaroo. The kangaroo gives Dot some magical "berries of understanding" that give her the Doolittlian ability to talk with the animals, and she embarks on an ecologically driven journey to understand humanity's negative impact on the natural environment. The interactive installation allows the audience to interact with the creatures and inhabit the digital world presented in the theater show. The experience begins without sound or projections, and as the audience traverses the seemingly empty space, digital particles are created from their movements, and the virtual bushland slowly emerges from the interactive floating particles. The magical shift from a disappointingly empty space to a fully fledged natural landscape through embodied interaction represents the eating of the berries and puts the audience into a state of "understanding" where they can begin their own transformative journey. Mirroring the surreal juxtaposition of real human participants with the surrounding virtual environment, the oversized interactive animals appear to possess a magical presence, simultaneously at one with their animated environment while exuding an almost-alien presence. The embodied interaction with these creatures physically echoes the relationship that human beings have with their own natural environment" (Bluff and Johnston, 2017a).

Figure 5.3: Participants can manipulate giant bird "totems" with their movement in Creature:Interactions. © Stalker Theatre. Photo: Andrew Bluff.

They explain that:

> "To provide the artwork with nuanced and expressive reactions to these free-form movements, the interaction aesthetic was driven by real-world physics simulations. In our design we favored 'continuous' gestural interaction where all movements of the participants result in the exertion of virtual forces on simulated physical objects in the virtual world. The intention is that this continuous, physical interaction leads to visual responses that are both complex and intuitively understandable, providing a rich scope for creative expression and discovery" (ibid).

> "The participants have a shared experience as they explore the digital environment and often form small groups…Live facilitators engage with children to suggest different forms of movement as they interact with the system and each other… The facilitators also form minigroups with the children to work together on tasks such as putting out a bushfire with imaginary buckets of water and hoses" (ibid).

One version of *Creature:Interactions* was stereoscopic, offering images in 3D space rather than just on the wall screens. Participant interaction was again studied and phantom physical effects were noticed when the:

> "... artwork features a large bushfire scenario that is eventually extinguished by a virtual rainstorm....in the 360° 2D installation, members of the audience reported that they could 'feel' the temperature drop during the virtual rain sequence, even though the actual temperature did not change. In addition to this cooling effect, some patrons of the stereoscopic 3D version described a heating effect during the bushfire sequence" (ibid).

When studying the closely related performance piece *Creature: Dot and the Kangaroo*, Bluff and Johnston (2017b) were able to collect reflections from the creative team as the work evolved as well as once it was complete. They found that certain scenes in the production were widely agreed to be successful, offering "peak experiences" in the production. So they looked into the nature of those peak moments. They observed that:

> "The peak scenes all contained a high density of every element, suggesting that an efficiency of language in any one medium was not crucial, but instead storytelling that occurred across many different elements produced more fruitful results. The coloured backgrounds and interactive totem graphics present through most of the performance described the location and spirit of the story but largely assumed the role of a 'living' digital set. In the more successful scenes identified, the system was designed to actually tell key moments of the text through interactive visual effects.... The interactive flocking of birds in the pigeon scene tell the story of nature's fear of humans and confirm the notion that Dot's actions have serious repercussions to the animals living in the natural bush environment.... The progressive disintegration of the dingo totem and splurging forth of bloody particles describes the gruesome nature of the kangaroo's triumphant victory to the audience. Rather than simply describing the location and spirit of each scene, the interactive system portrays key elements of the narration during the peak scenes elevating it's role from one of a digital set to become a true storytelling device.

The peak scenes of the show also contained the rare instances of actors acknowledging or actively interacting with the large projection screen. This deliberate interaction between human and digital suggests that the story is being told by both mediums in combination and permits the audience to focus attention on the connection between performer and digital environment. The berries and brolga scenes also link the performers movements to the animated landscape visuals through interactive visual effects. This coupling allows the particle and pre-rendered graphics to work in unison with the actors and briefly prevents the cognitive separation of background, foreground and performer that is present through most of the show" (Bluff and Johnston, 2017b).

5.4.1   LESSONS

• When groups of people (children in this case) interact with a system the resulting interactions between the people can be quite as significant as the HCI. As we saw earlier with *Iamascope*, an important issue can be the interactions between people that happen concurrently with interactions with computer-based systems. Studies of this situation are conducted in HCI but should, perhaps, be central to many more HCI investigations.

• Phantom physical experiences can be induced and may be as significant as real ones. The phenomena that we look for need to include phantom ones as well as physically measurable ones.

• In an interactive performance the visual effects can be a strong element in the story telling. Our experiences can be influenced by a wide range of factors. This is where context, for example, can be crucial in influencing what we see, hear, feel, or understand. As many researchers have pointed out in recent times, designing or selecting the context can be quite as important as designing the direct HCI features of a system.

CHAPTER 6

Conclusion:
The Next HCI Vocabulary

Where has this discussion led us?

Whereas a painter might be able to think in terms of hue, texture and so on, the interactive artist needs in addition to think in terms of forms of engagement, behaviours, and other considerations. Colour, for example, is hard enough to work with, but we know much more about it than about interaction. For that reason, the role of research within creative practice involving interaction is vitally important. Practice-based research in art, particularly in interactive art, has a direct relevance to HCI. My argument throughout this book is that HCI needs to take notice of what art is discovering and inventing and will, I believe, benefit from learning the lessons from art.

In making interactive art, the artist deals with the same issues and faces much the same challenges as in any other kind of art. However, each form and each medium has its own set of specific problems, and here interactive behaviour and engagement is key. For the artist, however, it is not necessarily a matter of coming to clear understanding of the issues involved but rather how to create works that challenge our assumptions and, in doing so, ask fundamental questions of us as human beings. This is, after all, the true role of art.

We see that a range of audience experience issues are important for the interactive artist and that research into them is a significant part of the art making process. A range of these issues has been identified, including a set of pleasure categories, an articulation of a developing engagement process, and different kinds of engagement over different periods of time. Artists are actively exploring both these factors and new methods that can be employed as part of artistic practice in order to deal with them. As I think I have made apparent in the discourse above, researchers in HCI and, in particular, experience design, would benefit from taking these art concerns into the study of interaction and user engagement.

The issues that have been presented are intended to initiate the development of a new language with which to discuss the characteristics of interaction well beyond art. Art can help us extend and refine the vocabulary that defines the topics that are important for research in HCI. The work described in this book can be used to frame a different kind of HCI research, one that focuses primarily on human values and augmenting human creativity.

This is, to my mind, one of the big challenges for our community and our time.

References

Apter, M. J. (1991). "A structural phenomenology of play," in Kerr, J. H. and Apter, M. J., Eds., *Adult Play: A Reversal Theory Approach*, Swets and Zeitlinger, Amsterdam, pp. 13–42. 49

Archer, B. (1995). "The nature of research," *Co-Design* January 6–13. Available at https://archive.org/details/TheNatureOfResearch. 18

Ascott, R. (1966). "Behaviourist art and the cybernetic vision." *Cybernetica*, 9: 247–264. 28, 37

Bann, S. (1970). *Experimental Painting*. Studio Vista, London. 13

Bell, S. (1991). "Participatory Art and Computers." Ph.D. Thesis: Loughborough University, UK. Available at http://nccastaff.bournemouth.ac.uk/sbell/. 34

Bently, T., Johnston, L., and Von Baggo, K. (2003). "Physiological responses during computer use," *Proceedings of the OzCHI2003*. CHISIG, Australia, pp. 174–182. 53

Berlyne, D. E. (1968). "Laughter, humor, and play," in Lindzey, G. and Aronson, E. eds. *The Handbook of Social Psychology*, Addison-Wesley, pp. 795–852. 49

von Betralanffy, L. (1950). "An outline of general systems theory," *The British Journal for the Philosophy Sci*ence, 1: 139–164. 28

von Bertalanffy, L. (1968). *General System Theory: Foundations, Development, Applications*. George Braziller, New York.

Bilda, Z., Edmonds, E., and Candy, L. (2008). "Designing for creative engagement," *Design Studies*, 29(6): 525–40. DOI: 10.1016/j.destud.2008.07.009. 55

Biles, K. (1994). "Notes on experience design," *ACM SIGGRAPH Computer Graphics*, 28(2): 145–146. DOI: 10.1145/178951.178979. 8

Bill, M. (1949). "The mathematical approach in contemporary art," *Werk* 3, (Winthertur, Switzerland, 1949); reprinted in Maldonado, T., (ed.) Max Bill, Buenos Aires, Argentina, 1955. 14

Bluff, A. and Johnston, A. (2017a). "Creature interactions: A social mixed-reality playspace," *Leonardo 50*(4): 360–367. DOI: 10.1162/LEON_a_01453. 59, 60

Bluff, A. and Johnston, A. (2017b). "Storytelling with interactive physical theatre: A case study of Dot and the Kangaroo," *Proceedings of the MOCO '17 4th International Conference on Movement Computing*, Article 19. ACM Press, New York. 59, 61, 62

Boden, M. A. (1991). *The Creative Mind: Myths and Mechanisms*. Basic Books, London. 9

Bollo, A. and Dal Pozzolo, L. (2005). "Analysis of visitor behaviour inside the museum: An empirical study," *Proceedings of the 8th International Conference on Arts and Cultural Management*, Montreal, July. 57

Bower, T. G. R. (1974). *Development in Infancy*. Freeman and Company, San Francisco, CA. 32

Caillois, R. (1962). *Man, Play, and Games*. Thames and Hudson, London. 49

Campbell-Johnston, R. (2008). "Mark Rothko at Tate Modern," *The Times*, London September 24. Available at http://entertainment.timesonline.co.uk/tol/arts_and_entertainment/visual_arts/article4811134.ece. (accessed March 22, 2010). 20

Candy, L. and Edmonds, E. A. (1996). "Introduction," in Candy, L. and Edmonds, E. A. eds., *Proceedings of Creativity and Cognition*, Loughborough University & Loughborough College of Art and Design, UK, pp. I–IV. 9

Candy, L. and Edmonds, E. A. (2002a). "Interaction in art and technology", *Crossings: Electronic Journal of Art and Technology* 2(1). Available at http://crossings.tcd.ie/issues/2.1/Candy/ (accessed April 28, 2017). 30

Candy, L. and Edmonds, E. A. (2002b). *Explorations in Art and Technology*. Springer-Verlag, London. DOI: 10.1007/978-1-4471-0197-0. 21

Candy, L. and Edmonds, E. A. (2002c). "The COSTART exhibition at C&C2002," *Proceedings of the Fourth Creativity & Cognition Conference: Exhibition Papers and Posters*, Mottram, J., Candy, L., and Kavanagh, T., eds., LUSAD Publications, Loughborough University, UK, pp. 11–22. 25

Candy, L. and Edmonds, E. A. (2018). "Practice-based research in the creative arts: Foundations and futures from the front line," *Leonardo*, 51(1): 63–69. DOI: 10.1162/LEON_a_01471. 18

Cornock, S. and Edmonds, E. A. (1970). "The creative process where the artist is amplified or superseded by the computer," *Proceedings of the Computer Graphics*

'70 Conference, Brunel University, UK and later published in a revised form in *Leonardo*, 16: 11–16 (1973). 28

Costello, B. (2007). "A pleasure framework," *Leonardo*, 40(4): 370–1. DOI: 10.1162/leon.2007.40.4.370. 47

Costello, B. (2009). "Gestural interfaces that stimulate creative play," Ph.D. thesis, University of Technology, Sydney. 49

Costello, B. and Edmonds, E. A. (2007). "A study in play, pleasure and interaction design," in *Proceedings of Designing Pleasurable Products and Interfaces*, (Helsinki, 2007), ACM Press, New York: 76–91. DOI: 10.1145/1314161.1314168. 49

Csikszentmihalyi, M. (1975). *Beyond Boredom and Anxiety: The Experience of Play in Work and Games.* Jossey-Bass Inc., San Francisco. 49

Csikszentmihalyi, M. (1996). *Creativity: Flow and the Psychology of Discovery and Invention.* Harper/CollinsNew York. 16

Doran, M. (ed) (2001). *Conversations with Cezanne,* University of California Press. 27

Dourish, P. (2001). *Where the Action Is: The Foundations of Embodied Interaction.* MIT Press, Cambridge, MA. 8

Duchamp, M. (1957). "The creative act," talk given in 1957 reprinted in *The Essential Writings of Marcel Duchamp*, Sanouillet, M. and Peterson, E., eds., Thames and Hudson, London, 1975, pp. 138–140. 20

Eco, U. (1962). *Opera Aperta.* In translation: *The Open Work*, Harvard University Press, Cambridge MA, 1989. 41

Edmonds, E. A. (1974). "A process for the development of software for non-technical users as an adaptive system," *General Systems XIX*, pp. 215–218. 27

Edmonds, E. A. (1975). "Art systems for interactions between members of a small group of people," *Leonardo*, 8: 225–227. DOI: 10.2307/1573243. 32

Edmonds, E. A. (1993). "Preface," in Candy, L. and Edmonds, E. A., eds., *Proceedings of Creativity and Cognition.* Loughborough University, UK, p. 1. DOI: 10.1159/000111329. 9

Edmonds, E. A. (2003). "Logics for constructing generative art systems," *Digital Creativity*, 14(1): 23–38. DOI: 10.1076/digc.14.1.23.8808. 34

Edmonds, E. A. (2006). "Abstraction and interaction: An art system for white noise," in *Computer Graphics, Imaging and Visualisation - Techniques and Applications*,

Banissi, E., et al., eds., IEEE Computer Society Conference Publishing Services, Los Alamitos, CA, pp. 423–427. 35, 57

Edmonds, E. A. (2007a). "Reflections on the nature of interaction," *CoDesign: International Journal of Co-Creation in Design and the Arts*, 3(3): 139–143. 35, 36

Edmonds, E. A. (2007b). *Shaping form: Generative Works Shaped by Interaction*, Creativity and Cognition Press, University of Technology, Sydney. 36

Edmonds, E. A. (2009). "Cities Tango: Between Belfast and Sydney, 2009," (installation), in Mey, K. E. A., ed., *ISEA: Interface*, University of Ulster, Belfast, Ireland. 37

Edmonds, E. A. (2011). "Interactive art," in Candy, L. and Edmonds, E. A., *Interacting: Art, Research and the Creative Practitioner*, Libri Press, Oxford, pp. 18–32. 20

Edmonds, E. A. and Quantrill, M. (1998). "An approach to creativity as process," *Proceedings of CAiiA Conference "Reframing Consciousness,"* Ascott, ed., Intellect Books, pp. 257–261. 34

Edmonds, E. A., Muller, L., and Connell, M. (2006). "On creative engagement," *Visual Communication*, 5(3): 307–322. DOI: 10.1177/1470357206068461. 56

Edmonds, E. A., Bilda, Z., and Muller, L. (2009). "Artist, evaluator and curator: three viewpoints on interactive art, evaluation and audience experience," *Digital Creativity*, 20: 141–151. DOI: 10.1080/14626260903083579. 52

Edmonds, E. and Candy, L. (2010). "Relating theory, practice and evaluation in practitioner research," *Leonardo*, 43(5): 470–476. DOI: 10.1162/LEON_a_00040. 18

Engelbart, D. C. (1967) "X-Y position indicator for a display system," U.S. patent 3,541,541. Available at http://web.stanford.edu/dept/SUL/library/extra4/sloan/MouseSite/Archive/patent/mousepatent.PDF (accessed April 27, 2017). 6

Ericsson, K. A. and Simon, H. A. (1993). *Protocol Analysis: Verbal Reports as Data*. MIT Press, Cambridge, MA. 53

Fels, S. and Mase, K. (1999). "Iamascope: a graphical musical instrument," *Computers & Graphics*, 23(2): 277–286. DOI: 10.1016/S0097-8493(99)00037-0. 23

Franco, F. (2018). *Generative Art: The Work of Ernest Edmonds*. Routledge, Abingdon, Oxfordshire. 27, 45

Galimberti, J. (2015). "The early years of GRAV: Better Marx than Malraux," *Own-Reality*, 13. Available at http://www.perspectivia.net/publikationen/ownreality/13/galimberti-en (accessed April 28, 2017). 14

Garneau, P. (2001). "Fourteen forms of fun," *Gama-sutra*. Available at http://www.gamasutra.com/view/feature/227531/fourteen_forms_of_fun.php (Accessed April 28, 2017). 49

Gero, J. S. and Maher, M. L. (eds.) (1989). "Preprints modeling creativity and knowledge-based creative design," Design Computing Unit, Department of Architectural and Design Science, University of Sydney, Sydney. 9

Gombrich, E. H. (1972). *The Story of Art* (12th ed.) Phaidon Press, London. 13

Gregory, R. L. (1974). *Concepts and Mechanisms of Perception*. Duckworth, London. 16

Groos, K. (1901). *The Play of Man*. William Heinemann, London. DOI: 10.1037/13084-000. 49

Gruden, G. (2016). *From Tool to Partner: The Foundation of Human-Computer Interaction*. Morgan & Claypool, San Rafael, CA. DOI: 10.2200/S00745ED-1V01Y201612HCI035. 8

Hunicke, R., LeBlanc, M., and Zubek, R. (2004). "MDA: A formal approach to game design and game research," in *Challenges in Game Artificial Intelligence: Papers from the 2004 AAAI Workshop*, (San Jose, CA, 2004), The AAAI Press, pp. 1–5. 49

IJMMS (2017). Available at http://www.sciencedirect.com/science/journal/00207373 (accessed April 27, 2017). 5

Isaacson, W. (2011). *Steve Jobs*. Little Brown, London. 6, 7, 8

Johnson, B. S. (1969). *The Unfortunates*. Panther Books, London. 28

Kachurin, P. (2013). *Making Modernism Soviet: the Russian Avant-Garde in the Early Soviet Era, 1918–1928*. Northwestern University Press, Evanston, IL. 14

Kay, A. (1972). "A personal computer for children of all ages," available at http://www.vpri.org/pdf/hc_pers_comp_for_children.pdf (accessed April 27, 2017). 6

Kirby, M. (1965). "Allan Kaprow's eat," *Tulane Drama Review*, 10(2): 44–49. DOI: 10.2307/1125230. 28

Khut, G. and Muller, L. (2005). "Evolving creative practice: A reflection on working with audience experience in Cardiomorphologies," in Anastasiuo, P., Smithies, R., Trist, K., and Jones, L., eds., *Vital Signs: Creative Practice & New Media Now*. RMIT Publishing, Melbourne, Australia. 38

Malone, T. W. (1982). "Heuristics for designing enjoyable user interfaces: Lessons from computer games," *Proceedings CHI'82*. ACM Press, New York, pp. 63–68. DOI: 10.1145/800049.801756. 8

Mauchly, J. W. (1973). "Preparation of problems for EDVAC-type machines," in Randell, B., ed., *The Origins of Digital Computers: Selected Papers.* (pp. 365–369). Berlin: Springer-Verlag, pp. 365– 369. 6

McRobert , L. (2007). *Char Davies's Immersive Virtual Art and the Essence of Spatiality*. University of Toronto Press, Toronto. DOI: 10.3138/9781442684171. 38

Muller, L., Edmonds, E. A., and Connell, M. (2006). "Living laboratories for interactive art," *CoDesign: International Journal of CoCreation in Design and the Arts*, 2(4): pp. 195–207. DOI: 10.1080/15710880601008109. 52, 53

Nakov, A. B. (2002). *Kazimir Malewicz: Catalogue raisonné*. Adam Biro, Paris. 13

Norman, D. (1988). *The Design of Everyday Things*. Doubleday, New York. 54

Norwich, K. H. (1982). "Perception as an active process," *Mathematics and Computers in Simulation*. 24(6): 535–553. DOI: 10.1016/0378-4754(82)90655-3. 20

Parkin, A. (1977). "Computing and people," papers submitted to the Conference at Leicester Polytechnic, December 20-22, 1976. Edward Arnold, London. 7

Pedley, E. (2014). *Dot and the Kangaroo*. Harper Collins Publishers, New York. 59

Popper, F. (2007). *From Technological to Virtual Art*. MIT Press, Cambridge, MA. 21

Reichardt, J. (ed.) (1968). "Cybernetic serendipity," Special Issue of *Studio International*, London. 15

Richards, M. (2008). "Why the iPhone makes 2008 seem like 1968 all over again," available at https://tinyurl.com/y7p3cmvj (accessed April 27, 2017). 6

Sandford, M. (1995). *Happenings and Other Acts (Worlds of Performance)*, Routledge, New York. 20

Schön, D. (1983). *The Reflective Practitioner*, Basic Books, New York. 19

Shackel, B. (1959). "Ergonomics for a computer," *Design*, 120: 36–39. 6, 7

Shackel, B. (1992). "HUSAT – 21 years of HCI: The Human Sciences & Advanced Technology Research Institute," *Proceedings of CHI1992*, ACM Press, New York, pp.282–283. DOI: 10.1145/142750.142811.

Shedroff, N. (2001). *Experience Design*. New Rider, Berkeley, CA. 55

Shneiderman, B. (1982). "The future of interactive systems and the emergence of direct manipulation," *Behaviour & Information Technology*, 1(3): 237–256. DOI: 10.1080/01449298208914450. 19

Shneiderman, B. (2016). *The New ABCs of Research: Achieving Breakthrough Collaborations*. Oxford. DOI: 10.1093/acprof:oso/9780198758839.001.0001. 18

Shneiderman, B., Fischer, G., Czerwinski, M., Resnick, M., Myers, B., Candy, L., Edmonds, E., Eisenberg, M., Giaccardi, E., Hewett, T., Jennings, P., Kules, B., Nakakoji, K., Nunamaker, J., Pausch, R., Selker, T., Sylvan, E., Terry, M. (2006). "White paper on creativity support tools workshop," *International Journal of Human Computer Interaction*, 20(2): 61–77. DOI: 10.1207/s15327590ijhc2002_1. 10

Sommerer, C. and Mignonneau, L. (2009). *Interactive Art Research*. SpringerWien, New York. 22, 23

Stalker Theatre, (2015). "*Creature: Dot and the Kangaroo*," available at http://www.stalker.com.au/creature. 59

Suchman, L. A. (1987). "Six vies of embodied cognition," *Psychonomic Bulletin Review*, 9(4): 625–636. 53

Sutherland, I. E. (1963). "SKETCHPAD, a man-machine graphical communication system," Ph.D. Thesis, MIT. 6

Treu, S. (ed.) (1976). *UODIGS '76 Proceedings of the ACM/SIGGRAPH Workshop on User-oriented Design of Interactive Graphics Systems*. ACM Press, New York. 7

Weizenbaum, J. (1966). "ELIZA — A computer program for the study of natural language communication between man and machine," *Communications of the ACM*, 9(1): 36–4. DOI: 10.1145/365153.365168. 31

Wiener, N. (1965). *Cybernetics*. MIT Press, Cambridge, MA. 28

Author's Biography

Ernest Edmonds is a pioneer computer artist and HCI innovator for whom combing creative arts practice with creative technologies has been a life-long pursuit. In 2017 he won both the ACM SIGCHI Lifetime Achievement Award for Practice in Human-Computer Interaction and the ACM SIGGRAPH Distinguished Artist Award for Lifetime Achievement in Digital Art. He is Chairman of the Board of ISEA International, whose main activity is the annual International Symposium on Electronic Art that began in 1988.

Ernest was born in London in 1942 and, having started at Leicester Polytechnic (now De Montfort University—DMU), he then worked at Loughborough University and the University of Technology, Sydney, before returning to DMU as Professor of Computational Art and Director of the Institute of Creative Technologies.

Ernest's art was already computer based before 1970, and his future vision was to transform user participation with interactive and distributed works. From that time he began a quest to transform user interface design to an adaptive and iterative process and by 1973 he had made HCI at Leicester Polytechnic a priority research area. From this work came some of the first published articles about interactive art (1970), iterative design methods (1974), user interface architectures (1982), and the support of creativity (1989). His books include *The Separable User Interface* (Academic Press), *Explorations in Art and Technology* (Springer), and *Interacting: Art, Research and the Creative Practitioner* (Libri), the last two co-authored with Linda Candy. A second revised edition *Explorations* is in press. In 1993, he co-founded the Creativity & Cognition conference series, a SIGCHI sponsored event since 1999. He is an Honorary Editor of *Leonardo* and Editor-in-Chief of Springer's *Cultural Computing* book series.

Over the last 50 years, Ernest has exhibited his artwork across the globe. In recent years, he has shown in Venice, Leicester, Denver, Beijing, Shanghai, and Rio de Janerio. He has previously shown in, for example, London, Sydney, Melbourne, Moscow, Riga, Rotterdam, Berlin, and Washington DC. The Victoria and Albert Museum London collects his art and archives. His work was recently described in the book by Francesca Franco, *Generative Systems Art: The Work of Ernest Edmonds* (Routledge, 2017).